```
D0867008
```

STRUCTURAL ANALYSIS OF NARRATIVE

THE SOCIETY OF BIBLICAL LITERATURE
SEMEIA SUPPLEMENTS
Edited by William A. Beardslee

STRUCTURAL ANALYSIS
OF NARRATIVE

by

Jean Calloud

Translated by

Daniel Patte

FORTRESS PRESS
Philadelphia, Pennsylvania

SCHOLARS PRESS
Missoula, Montana

Translated from the French, by Daniel Patte and with permission of
the publisher, *L'Analyse Structurale du Récit* by Jean Calloud
(Lyon: Profac, 1973).

English translation Copyright © 1976 by The Society of Biblical
Literature

Library of Congress Catalog Card Number 75-37158

ISBN 0-8006-1503-4

5416E76   Printed in the U.S.A.   1-1503

TABLE OF CONTENTS

PART II: Temptation of Jesus
in the Wilderness
Structural Analysis of a Narrative

Translator's Preface

Jean Calloud's book is an introduction to the structural analysis of narrative as practiced by A. J. Greimas and his disciples in his seminar at L'Ecole Pratique des Hautes Etudes (Paris). This setting for Greimas' teaching and writings must be kept in mind for a proper understanding of his published work as well as of Calloud's book. Professor Greimas' primary goal is the training of "scholars" or, better, of "scientists." He invites his students to join him in a theoretical scientific research in semantics.

The first results of this ongoing research make it possible to affirm that at least some features of the so elusive meaning of a text can be captured in the net of a rigorous scientific method. Literary critics and biblical scholars can no longer ignore this claim. If it is true, their disciplines will necessarily be affected by it. They must evaluate for themselves this research which promises what they take to be the realization of an impossible dream. But how could they evaluate it when the available literature on structuralism is either purely theoretical or unreadable because of its technical jargon! Calloud provides us with a true introduction. His book does not presuppose, on the reader's part, any knowledge of the linguistic technical terminology, and yet does not compromise the scientific rigor of the method. Calloud achieves this remarkable result by focusing on the method for the analysis of a specific type of text, the narrative, and by providing a detailed example in which he shows, step by step, how one can proceed with such an analysis. Despite the clarity of Calloud's text, a few comments on the context in which Greimas developed this theoretical scientific research in semantics might be useful for the reader of this translation.

The rigor and even the methods of this scientific research are and must be comparable to those of physicists and other scientists. Such a strict approach characterizes structural linguistics and semiology. Yet the linguists (such as E. Benveniste) have emphasized — and are still emphasizing — that this *science* of signs is strictly limited to the study of discrete elements of language: the signs. A system of signs can be rigorously analyzed as can other features of language (such as its phonetic system and its grammar), because this system is shared by all of the participants in a culture (or sub-culture). Each sign has a "value" which is its interrelation with the other signs of the system. The network of these semiotic interrelations can be the object of a structural investigation. By contrast, larger linguistic units such as discourses or narratives do not lend themselves to a rigorous analysis. They belong to the semantic level (as contrasted with the semiotic level), that is, to language in its function as mediator between man and his world. This level of linguistic communication is exclusively characterized by the "enunciation." The term "enunciation" (Fr. *énonciation*) designates the creative use that the speaker makes of the language in function of his situation in life and of his intentionality. The speaker transforms the signs into words by ascribing to each sign a specific referent which is selected from among the possibilities offered by the system of signs. He creates ever new sentences (which are semantic units like the words and not semiotic units like the signs) by making use of the possibilities offered by the grammar of this language. Beyond the sentence level the speaker's discourse is free from any linguistic and semiotic constraints. The specific combination of sentences in the discourse exclusively manifests the interaction of the speaker with his "situation in life" (this phrase must be understood in a broad sense so as to include everything from the speaker's culture down to his interlocutors). Each discourse is unique. Therefore, speaking of the linguistic or structural laws which govern the creation of discourses is a contradiction in terms. This briefly summarizes Benveniste's argument (cf. E. Benveniste, *Problèmes de Linguistique Générale* II, Paris, Gallimard, 1974, 215-38).

Structural semantics is possible. This claim is made explicit in the very titles of Greimas' books: *Sémantique structurale* (Paris, Larousse, 1966) and *Du Sens. Essais Sémiotiques* (Paris, Seuil, 1970). For him, discourses are themselves under structural or semiotic constraints. Greimas' research encompasses a variety of types of discourses; let us focus on one of them, the narrative.

Many different discourses are immediately recognized as having the value "narrativity" (i.e., as being meaningful narrative). This recognition is linked neither to a specific culture — a narrative can be translated — nor to a specific mode of expression — the value narrativity can at once be manifested in natural languages, in mimes, in movies, in paintings, etc. This observation led Greimas to postulate that there are additional constraints. If we consider a narrative text, in addition to the linguistic constraints, there are broader, transcultural constraints which he terms the narrative structures. He uses the plural form to express the complexity of the network of relations. The singular form can be used to emphasize the universality of this network.

Without entering into the philosophical debate about its metaphysical status, let us simply say that the narrative structure is a specific way to interrelate semantic units. It is common to all narratives in all cultures and is also presupposed by anyone able to recognize meaningful narratives — that is, any human being. The verification of this postulate is a matter of scientific research.

The structural analyst's project is similar to that of the physicist. Both are confronted with a phenomenon which appears as an atom, that is, as an indivisible entity. An atom of hydrogen has specific properties (e.g., its weight) which, when listed, appear to describe the nature of this atom in contrast to any other atom.

The meaning of a narrative may be understood as an "atom." Its specific characteristics or properties are bonded together into an apparently indivisible entity because they are viewed as manifestations of the author's thought. It seems that the "nature" of the meaning of that narrative can only be defined in contrast to the meanings of other narratives.

By breaking the atom into particles and sub-particles the physicist attempts to show that the atom's properties can be explained by universal laws. If I may risk a simple (and certainly simplistic) example, some of the properties of an atom may be explained by the relations among protons, neutrons, and electrons. The laws which govern these relations (the relational structure), are constants, i.e., they apply to any atom. The characteristics of each atom are then explained by the number and kind of particles which it contains, i.e., in structural terms, by the specific investment of the relational structure.

Similarly, the structural analyst must break the atom "meaning-of-a-narrative" into semantic units in the hope of explaining the semantic specificity of each narrative as the specific investment of a relational structure which is common to all narratives.

How should the meaning of a narrative be broken up? There are many possible types of semantic units: sentences, groups of sentences, phrases, speech units, lexies, etc. What are the "pertinent" semantic units? That is, what are the semantic units which, through their interrelation, display the relational laws which characterize any narrative? In this quest for the pertinent semantic units and for the pertinent relations the analyst must keep in mind that the structure as a relational network is a *constant* which is in itself semantically empty and is only manifested when invested by *variable* semantic features. Thus the analysis must reduce the variables in order that the structure might be uncovered. The analyst must also keep in mind that a narrative or an atom is only a partial investment of the total relational network.

A study of the narrative structure is, therefore, a form of scientific research which must proceed as in any theoretical research. A theoretical model (a "prevision" as Calloud says) is first conceived by the scientist, then verified by experimentation. According to the experimental results, this model is either completely discarded or revised and then submitted to new verification. This long process reaches its goal when a model appears to be an adequate representation of the phenomenon under study. It nevertheless remains a model which is always open to revision if new data demand it.

A model for a part of the narrative structure has been established by Greimas and his disciples. This has been termed the syntactic structure but is often referred to as "the narrative structure." This first and important result is not an end in itself. It opens up the possibility for new theoretical investigation. Are there universal laws which govern the investments of the syntactic structure? What are the relations between the syntactic structure and the enunciation? Calloud terms this second step in the research "analysis of semantic contents." Even beyond this, a similar structural research must be applied to other forms of discourse (e.g., philosophical and juridical discourses) and to other modes of human communication (e.g., plastic arts). Professor Greimas and his seminar are presently involved in this latest stage of research.

From the above remarks it is clear that Professor Greimas' teaching and writings aim at uncovering the semantic structures. This is a form of theoretical scientific research as contrasted with practical research aimed at developing concrete uses of this theoretical knowledge. Greimas teaches a scientific method adequate for such a theoretical research and not a method which could be directly employed in practical application. Similarly, he is not interested in the meaning of a text *per se* but only that it is a manifestation of semantic structures. This simple fact has frequently been overlooked by biblical scholars who, when confronted by the structural methods of Greimas or other structural scholars, were quite disappointed by the results of tedious analyses which did not bring forth any new insight with respect to the meaning of a text. Indeed, these methods were aimed at something else! However, these methods of theoretical research have been used for the practical purpose of interpreting texts, especially in literary studies. We can understand why their methodology was often judged to be dubious at once by the more rigorous structural scholars and by the scholars using traditional methods, despite their fascinating results.

Father Jean Calloud, professor of Old Testament at the "Faculté de théologie" (Université catholique de Lyon) and at the "Centre théologique de Meylan" (Grenoble), together with a group of French exegetes headed by Professor Jean Delorme, remains quite convinced of the exegetical and hermeneutical promise of the results of structural research. Yet they are quite aware that Greimas' structural methods are *not* exegetical methods. In terms of the preceding analogy, it is quite clear that the engineer who is involved in a research aimed at creating, let us say, a nuclear reactor, is not using the physicist's methods. Rather, his own methods are built on the theoretical knowledge which results from the physicist's research. Thus he must acquire a detailed understanding of this theoretical knowledge by studying how the physicist reached his conclusions. As exegete, Calloud aims at using the results of theoretical structural research for a pragmatic purpose: a better understanding of the biblical text. New exegetical methods, structural exegesis, are cautiously being developed on the basis of the structural models which are sufficiently established (cf. Daniel Patte, *What is Structural Exegesis?*, Philadelphia: Fortress Press, 1976). Yet their development and practice demand a solid understanding of the nature of these models and, therefore, of how these models have been established. In the first part of his book, Calloud introduces the reader to the method of *theoretical* structural research so as to permit a clear understanding of the model proposed by Greimas of the syntactic narrative structure. Then, in the second part of the book, he makes use of this established model in the analysis of the story of the temptation of Jesus in the wilderness in order to show the interrelation of various semantic features of this text. By contrast, when dealing with the "analysis of semantic contents" in his first part Calloud cannot propose a complete model of the laws which govern the investments of the syntactic structure. Research is still in process at that level. Nevertheless certain structural characteristics of the personages as narrative figures have been identified. Calloud uses them for the analysis of his text. In so doing he isolates a number of semantic categories. The exegetical and hermeneutical implications of this analysis become visible. Yet he refuses to draw any conclusions. His analysis is, in his words, "a methodological quest." At this second level, he analyzes the text with a tentative and partial model as opposed to an established model. This model is adequate for this specific text, yet it must still be refined and verified by carrying out additional analyses and must be complemented so that it will account for other aspects of the semantic investment of the syntactic narrative structure.

Reading Calloud's book, we are therefore invited to take the first necessary steps toward structural exegetical methods while being warned that their development is dependent upon further theoretical research. Several exegetes presently participate in this theoretical research, rather than waiting passively for the results of other scholars' work. Calloud is one of them.

A first draft of this translation was available to my seminar at Vanderbilt University. Brenda Hopson, John Jones, Ed MacMahon, Judson Parker, and Gary Phillips have significantly contributed to its improvement by many suggestions. I am much indebted to them as well as to Professor William Beardslee for his careful editorial work on the manuscript, and to John Dominic Crossan for editorial suggestions, although I have to assume the responsibility for this translation.

Daniel Patte
Vanderbilt University

Part I

Elements of a Method

Introduction

When confronted with a meaningful text, our first reaction is to assume that meaning is natural and that it offers itself as a whole which cannot be deconstructed. Yet structural semantics affirms that meaning is an "effect." It results from the organization of elements less complex than the meaning perceived in reading. Thus, meaning is an effect that one can deconstruct to show how it is built. Without this irreverent attitude toward meaning, one remains in a mythical perspective in which meaning is a revered idol. The modern attitude toward discourse is iconoclastic of this idol. The structuralist movement as a whole invites us to reconstruct meaning, using a method which allows us to take apart the figures of meaning. Thus, a structural analysis is a quite peculiar study of meaning.

The following pages do not pretend to give a complete exposition of this science of signification called "semiotics." Neither do they intend to be a complete presentation of the presuppositions, limitations, and procedures of this science. This text would like to be an introduction to the method. What should one do in order to analyze how meaning is constructed in a text? What are the procedures and the operations that one needs to perform?

The testing field chosen for this analysis is the story of the temptations of Jesus in the wilderness. But structural analysis is not the biblical exegete's alone. It is concerned with any human discourse through which man produces and exchanges meaning. Both the theologian who constructs a discourse about God, and the patrologist who studies the discourse of the Tradition, should be concerned to know the conditions which preside over the production of such discourses and how they function. As E. Güttgemanns wrote, "If therefore the discourse about God is the sole positive 'data' which theological science has, one must conclude that theology must (and cannot avoid to) join specific sciences which are parts of the scientific endeavor as a whole and which have been recently termed 'science of the text.'"

The very phrase, "science of the text," implies a strict and demanding succession of operations which guarantees the integrity of such a scientific endeavor applied to texts. These pages are an invitation to this scientific quest.

Chapter I

Problematic

In order to undertake a fruitful structural analysis of narrative, it is necessary to understand its aim and its procedure, i.e., the *series of operations which have to be performed* in a specific order. Such an analysis begins with a text which may be readable and yet hides the rules of its game. It ends when a SYSTEM or an immanent STRUCTURE is brought to light. Because it is immanent, such a structure is "distant" from the "surface" of the text. What we designate by the term "structure" should not be identified with the "plan" nor with the "breaking down of the text into reading units" (paragraphs, verses, or lexies), nor again with the classification of semantic contents. The structural description implies the passing over from concrete statements, as manifested in the text in a specific language and style, to abstract units capable of being elements of a "system." Such a system finds its coherence in an interplay of relations defined without reference to any concrete realization. The textual statements (that we shall call "lexies") are the end-product of the operations through which the discourse has been produced. They represent neither the structure nor the "competence" (i.e., the use that somebody is able to make of a structure, tr.). The textual statements are rather "occurrence" and "performance." A study of the text at this level is not structural. By contrast, the operations of ANALYSIS are aimed, so to speak, at textual "models" kept in a "locus" far removed from the texts. In this locus everything is rigorously logical. Nothing escapes from the network of relations. It is from this remote locus that texts spring forth. The actual texts may seem fanciful and strange variations of the "models." One may have the feeling that they are free from any constraints imposed by a formal network of relations. Nevertheless, any meaningful text remains tied down by a discrete thread to an imposed "program." The procedure that we shall define below corresponds to the journey from the surface of the text to this locus which regulates the production of discourses. It is an exploratory and descriptive journey in a quasi-unknown territory for which we have very tentative maps showing nothing but a few landmarks and dotted lines which suggest possible trails connecting these landmarks. Certainly, there are several possible procedures, several possible ways in this territory. There are indeed several possible routes from one landmark to another, and also we may want to reach a locus different from the one sought by other "explorers of the structure." This pluralism of theories about the text and, hence, of analytical methods is characteristic of the present stage of semiotic research and demands that we examine carefully the problem and denounce the false innocence of any operation performed on texts before describing a specific procedure.

A. FROM STRUCTURAL LINGUISTICS
TO DISCOURSE ANALYSIS

Discourse analysis aims at exploring the SYSTEM underlying the manifestation (the text as it presents itself to the reader) in the same way as linguistics delineates the structure of "language" through an analysis of "speech" (*parole*). Thus discourse analysis (or semiotics) and structural linguistics have similar goals, procedures, and methodological concepts. This proximity can temporarily help to prepare the interpreter for textual analysis. Nevertheless, one should not overlook the specificity of discourse analysis as description of texts as compared with linguistic analysis as description of sentences. Recent theoretical and procedural developments in semiotic research tend to widen the gap between "linguistic grammar" and "theory of discourse." The young "science of the text" is more and more viewed as autonomous from linguistics. Even though our view of narrative structures is still significantly informed by a linguistic model, we presuppose on the basis of V. Propp's, R. Barthes', and A. J. Greimas' research that beside and beyond the linguistic system, there is a system which accounts for the overall organization of a textual surface. We presuppose also the possibility of reconstituting this system from the various occurrences. Taking this first methodological option separates us from those for whom the sole system underlying the discourse is the linguistic system which is manifested at the level of the sentence. In this other view, structural constraints are limited to the sentence level: the speaker exercises his freedom by combining sentences to produce discourse, which is held to belong exclusively to the level of "speech" (*parole*) and to be open to stylistic analysis only.

By constrast, we apply to discourse the notion of "system" which F. de Saussure used in order to define "language." In so doing we postulate a locus of constraints which characterizes the discourse as discourse. Language was viewed by de Saussure as a "closed system of signs." Similarly for us, the text is a "closed system," a "structured space" to be distinguished from the manifestation. This postulates that there are "meaning-producing" operations (*opérations de "signifiance"*) which can be identified and analyzed at the level of *discourse* but not at the level of the *sentence*. In other words, beyond the lexematic level (i.e., beyond individual statements) and beyond the syntagmatic level (i.e., beyond the succession of statements in the textual manifestation), there are "clusters of meaning" which can be accounted for only when the discourse as a whole is taken into consideration. This posits the need for an analysis (distinct from linguistic analysis) which would permit the reconstitution of a "pre-, para-, or sub-textual space." Such a designation is a metaphor. It corresponds to a representation of the text as "volume" and suggests the following polarities: "Immanence vs. Manifestation," "Deep Structure vs. Surface Structure," "Deep Grammar vs. Surface Grammar . . . " [vs. (read "versus") is intended to account for the semantic relation in its twofold aspect of discontinuity and of continuity, of conjunction and disjunction]. This metaphor opens the possibility of distinguishing between what belongs to the strict and closed organization of the "competence" (structural level) and what belongs to the indefinite interplay of the "performances" (surface level). Yet this metaphor does not imply any value judgment.

When the possibility of viewing discourse as a "system" of communication is accepted, we need to define the minimal units which constitute the system, and which actually are units of communication. We can expect to find that these units exist in two forms or, more specifically, that they have a twofold identity. They can be defined in terms of two types of relations since they can be projected either on a formal "grid" or on a surface of manifestation. An example proposed by F. de Saussure explains this last remark. A fifty-franc bill may represent a part of the sum of money paid in exchange for some goods and it may simultaneously represent, outside any specific use, the intermediary "value" between the ten-franc bill and the one hundred-franc bill in the French monetary system. The *uses* of the bill and the operations which can be performed at this level (addition, subtraction, multiplication . . .) presuppose the definition of its "value." In both cases (the case of the money and that of the text), there is the possibility for the user to pass in either direction from one level to the other. It is equally possible for what is manifested as "unit of speech" (*parole*) in a text to be converted into "unit of system" (whether language or discourse system). Conversely, what is learned as (linguistic or narrative) "competence" can be used and therefore transcribed into sentences and discourses.

What does the metaphor of the "conversions" represent? How can one perform such "conversions" from the text to the system? Such are the questions with which we shall deal. Then we shall be able to speak of an "analytic" competence.

B. PREVISION OF THE SYSTEM

Like any set of "game rules," the system of discourse, or the systems corresponding to the various genres, can be reconstituted from the actual texts and be described. If these systems were known, the work of the analyst would be comparable to that of the crossword puzzle devotee who has a "grid" in which he can transcribe the words corresponding to the list of definitions, and in so doing he can verify his answers. Yet our knowledge of the discourse system is still very partial and hypothetical. Consequently, the analyst's quest in the present state of research must be tentative. At the outset of his research, the analyst needs to envision (or, better, to "pre-vision") what is the general framework (or at least some features) of the system. In the process of the analysis he will refine, modify, correct, and even re-design completely this rough model of the system that he had "pre-visioned."

Let us proceed to this "pre-vision of the system." On this basis, we shall make some general observations which will progressively introduce us into the "structural universe," or, more specifically, into the spirit of the proposed method.

(1) Envisioned as analogous to the linguistic system, the text system can be expected to include:

a morphology

a syntax

a semantics

In other words, the text system is made up of units which are defined and classified (morphology) and which can be combined by following a number of rules (syntax). As a result of such combinations these units are capable of producing various "meaning effects" ("*effets de sens*": semantics). These units belong to various levels. These levels are interrelated according to a hierarchy which has to be respected when passing from one level to the other. On the basis of this first observation we shall distinguish between (a) morpho-syntactic structures and (b) semantic contents. Specific "models" correspond to each of these two levels. The relevance of these categories will be verified at the end of our presentation.

(2) In order to be truly "structural," the text system must be exclusively relational. In it there cannot be any self-contained term, any fixed point. Everything must be defined in terms of relation. In some instances, for clarity's sake, or in order to go directly to the point, or again because of our limited ability to pursue the analysis, we may be led to presuppose basic terms

which cannot be divided or converted into relations. In such cases we shall have to acknowledge that the "system" resulting from such an investigation remains problematic and tentative. This principle guides and gives impetus to the analysis. Not to apply this principle is the most common weakness in structural analysis. The most recent essays are characterized by its more rigorous application.

Let us emphasize the practical consequence of the preceding comment. The analyst must expose the relational, thus the "construct," character of the text. This relational character is hidden in and by the manifestation which gives to the text a "substantial" and "natural" appearance. The more one remains on the surface of the text, the more its elements seem to have meaning in themselves: it seems that they can be defined totally in terms of their own content. Is this not how we perceive words in a statement? By contrast, the more one considers a text in terms of structure, the more the units are broken down and disclose their relational status and their participation in an endless network of correlations in which "everything is difference."

C. FROM THE PREVISION OF THE SYSTEM TO THE ANALYSIS

Whenever a text is produced by making use of the system, the illusion of "self-contained content" is generated. Thus, we can conceive of the relations of the structure with the textual surface according to the model of a "filling-up" process, or of a "fixation" and "solidification" process. In this process the relational aspect characteristic of the system is hidden, giving way to "content effect" or "meaning effect." We shall see below how to refine this first representation.

What is constructed in this way and, thus, what must be de-constructed by the analyst in order to account for the place in the system of each unit? What is the process (and thus what is the sequence of steps) which presides over the transformation of a system into a textual manifestation? This process and this sequence define the landmarks which will guide the journey of the explorers from the textual to (and into) the structure. What is the inter-relationship of the elements which contribute to the generation of the discourse when they are combined into larger units? What figures are perceived when these relations are analyzed? Which elements are involved? What types of combinations give a specific shape to the message over against a background of differences? Both the multiplicity of these questions and the need to consider them at several levels suggest that the analysis will be *progressive*. The discourse system involves a number of levels which must be defined not only in themselves but also in terms of their conditions of integration.

In the following pages these methodological considerations will be made explicit and translated into a concrete procedure.

D. PRACTICAL ADVICE

The structural analysis of texts is difficult. Each of its operations involves uncertainty and risk. Yet it seems that all the difficulties are gathered together in the first step. This is to say that the fate of the analysis is decided in the first operation. We want to speak of the crucial moment when one leaves aside the textual surface, when one abandons its reassuring "self-sufficiency," its obvious content, in order to posit the general outline of the system. Sometimes one does not know how to begin. Roland Barthes pointed out this difficulty in an article published in the journal *Poétique* (1, 1970, 3-9) entitled, "Par où commencer?" It is essential to avoid any confusion with the approach of other methods (this is especially important for those who are used to practicing "literary criticism," "historical criticism," or any other "genetic" method). In order to orient correctly one's research, it may be helpful to ask the question: "*What happens in the text?*" Not in the life setting or time of its composition . . . not in the mind or subconscious of the author . . . not in the rest of his work

... but in the specific section of text under examination. This question may be surprising for somebody who has never considered a text as a stage on which something could "happen" ... for somebody who has never acknowledged that *logical operations* (such as affirmation, negation, conjunction, disjunction, attribution, modalization, etc.) are in their own ways "happenings." Yet, is it surprising that the realities are linguistic in the linguistic field? This question, when kept in mind, should prevent any confusion and permit the first steps toward the uncovering of the system underlying the statement. Actually, this question is nothing more than the "principle of immanence," a principle which is the very foundation of any structural method.

CONCLUSION

What was the purpose of these preliminary remarks? Their sole purpose was to create a "distance" between the object and the method. As a brief statement of the presuppositions of the method, they are what must be rejected if one does not agree with the following presentation. For, indeed, there is no innocent method — quite to the contrary, every method presupposes a theory of text and this theory must be constantly reevaluated. It was necessary to refer briefly to some of our presuppositions, both in order to provide a basis for the method and to submit the presupposed theory to the critical evaluation of the reader.

Chapter II

Morpho-Syntactic Structures of Narrative

In order to describe the procedure of analysis, it is necessary to adopt the attitude of an analyst, i.e., of somebody confronted with an oral or written narrative text. At first, we consider this text exclusively as *statement* (*énoncé*) (or set of statements). Indeed, this text reflects also the intersubjective conditions which presided over its enunciation (*énonciation*), i.e., its production. Yet, at least in its first phase, our method demands that we bracket out the enunciation (which is not without creating a number of problems that we shall deal with below). Thus, the text appears as a succession of statements or of sentences which are built according to the rules of a specific language and related to each other according to some kind of "logic."

The common operation performed on the text is *reading*. There is no problem here. All the literate users of a language are able to do it. A text is to be read, a discourse to be heard. As a result of reading the text is more or less understood, and in most instances sufficiently so: a second reading is not necessary. Sometimes, we need a shorter, more schematic representation of the text. In such cases we proceed to establish the plan which divides the textual surface in terms of the "joints" of the content apprehended during the reading. Such a plan is often proposed by the author or the editor and suggested with the help of titles, subtitles, indentations, paragraphs, and sometimes suggested further by literary and stylistic features. All this is useful, but it is not yet structural analysis. The units of reading are words, propositions, and sentences. Grammatical and logical analyses permit the explication of difficult passages. It should be emphasized that the procedure which we are presenting here presupposes such an "intelligent reading." It would not be possible to perform a structural analysis by studying a non-deciphered signifier. (This need for "meaning" at the starting point of a structural analysis raises, of course, a number of questions. It is in order to attempt to overcome this problem that methods related to "distributionalism" have been developed in parallel with structural methods: it is an attempt to find criteria which would be independent of meaning).

A structural analysis does not deal with these various units of the surface of the text. It rather deals with units which represent the elementary operations of the signification. These units can be interrelated in a purely formal manner. However, this formal interrelation of structural units does not constitute the manifested text, but rather its "model." The narrative structural model represents the rules which preside over the creation of the narrative as a whole (just as the linguistic structural model represents the rules which preside over the creation of each sentence).

A. FROM "LEXIE" TO CANONIC NARRATIVE STATEMENT

a) The "lexie"

In the first phase of his research the analyst must work with units which belong to the level of *reading*. The "lexie" is a unit of reading. It is not yet a unit of the system. It is a part of the text, which can include several sentences, or a single sentence, or again only part of a sentence. According to Roland Barthes' definition, it is "the best possible space in which one can apprehend meaning" (cf. Oswald Ducrot et Tzvetan Todorov, *Dictionnaire Encyclopédique des Sciences du Langage*. Paris: Le Seuil, 1972, 280). Dividing the text into lexies does not modify the text surface. It is done on the basis of a simple reading which suggests the obvious meaning and notes the interrelation of textual units. A definition of the lexie in terms of its minimal scope could be that in this textual space something must happen. Yet, there should not be too many "happenings" in it — otherwise, its interpretation will be difficult. In a lexie, each "happening" is the creation of a relation. For instance, something happens when an actor (or "personage") is related to another actor (or to himself, or to an inanimate oject, or, again, to a quality) by means of a verb (or one of its substitutes). "Peter meets Paul." "Peter laughs at himself." "Peter enjoys Paul's visit." "Paul receives a gift." "Paul is tall, bad." Although the delimitation of the lexies is not difficult and does not require one to imagine other forms of the text, there are sometimes a few problems. The analyst needs to make explicit what is elliptic or condensed; he needs to reduce the paraphrases and to reconstruct the deep order of the sentence (for instance, a passive form must be converted into an active form; a pronominal form into a nominal form . . .). When this is done, the text appears as a large piece of material in which are interwoven two or three types of threads: the actors, the processes, and the qualifications (processes and qualifications can be viewed as belonging together). The lexies can also be classified into two categories: function and qualification (these categories correspond to the classical pair narration/description). Furthermore, some of the features of the enunciation (*énonciation*) can be noted for their own sake: use of the first person and/or of the second person; deictics ("this, that, these, those, here, now, today . . ."); comparisons; evaluations . . . On the basis of this first filtering and classification, the analyst can record, in a slightly normalized form, the "happenings" of the text. Then, on the basis of this transcription, he can make a few reductions in order to begin to elicit the constants and the variables which are manifested in the text. "Peter strangles Paul" can be registered in two quasi-equivalent ways:

> "Subject: Peter-Process: Strangle-Object: Paul"
> "Subject: Peter-Process: Attack-Object: Paul"
> (Process: Kill)
> Similarly: "Peter gives his book to Paul"
> "Subject: Peter-Process: gives-Object: book
> Process: communicate + Paul"

One should not spend too much time on this first stage of the procedure. It is better to begin as soon as possible the series of operations which are aimed at defining the system network. It should be clear that in practice the analysis progresses simultaneously at several levels: often, obscure points at one level will be clarified by means of an anticipation of the following steps.

Let us emphasize that the elements which constitute the lexie are the *actors* and the *processes*.

b) Canonic Narrative Statements

We can now being to identify or, better, to construct the "canonic narrative statements." By this phrase we denote the elementary syntactic forms manifested in the lexies. The word "statement" (*énoncé*) is *not* to be understood here, as it is by some linguists (for instance, John Lyons in *Introduction to Theoretical Linguistics*, Cambridge, 1968), to mean "unit of speech" (*parole*) to be contrasted with "sentence" as "unit of language." By the term "statement," we rather designate a unit of *narrative grammar*. Thus, it must be carefully distinguished from the "linguistic statements" which constitute the textual surface. *Narrative* statement constitutes the minimal formal framework in which the basic elements of the "narrative grammar" can be manifested and interrelated. Such basic elements are, among others, the *Actants* and the *Functions*. Thus, the term "narrative statement" connotes the combination of at least two basic elements. This is why we can call it a "syntactic unit." In the closed boundaries of the statement the simplest correlation of elements takes place. These basic elements are defined by their ability to become associated with each other according to the rules of the narrative syntax. Furthermore, these statements are said to be *canonic* in order to distinguish them clearly from the "linguistic statements" because they are defined by means of abstract and general features. Each *canonic* statement can be the model and the generator of a great number of concrete linguistic statements.

The canonic narrative statements have fixed forms. Their coherence is defined by specific types of relations (structural relations characteristic of a given system which are consequently independent of the variables which permit their manifestations). *These relations are invariants.* This explains their importance for the analysis of discourse. Their invariance exists at the syntactic level: it results from the constraint which sets the basic elements of discourse into specific interrelations inside each type of statement. Secondarily, their invariance belongs to the semantic level insofar as the semic investment of these basic elements is sufficiently weak that it can remain stable inside a "genre" (the variations produce a few well determined "classes"). It is essential for the analyst to be able to construct these canonic statements out of the linguistic statements given in the lexies. This is a crucial and difficult step in the procedure.

Through his study of the lexies the analyst can take note of the correlations which constitute at the surface of the text the meaning apprehended in reading. The result is a list of *processes* performed by the actors and upon the actors. As long as we use the *verbs* to designate the processes, this list of processes is quite heterogeneous. Each process differs from the others, even though some similarity may already appear here or there (by the use of the same verbs or of synonymous verbs . . .). This is because we listed all of the variables. Are we not accustomed to "varying" as much as possible the terms of our discourses in order to avoid monotony and repetitions? Here a stylistic quality is an obstacle for the analysis. By contrast, the list of *actors* is shorter and points more directly to the "constants" of the text. Necessarily, the personages seem more stable than the processes, if for no other reason than that they are "covered up" by a proper noun (and the less the noun is meaningful, the more stable it is).

The first operation consists of *reducing* the great number of variables to a few invariants. This is an operation of classification (the technical books often call it a "taxonomy"). A knowedge of the "classes" of processes which have been established as a result of the analyses performed by various scholars will greatly facilitate this classification. The "geography" of these common bases from which the manifested processes are derived, permits the above-mentioned prevision of the system. This prevision is often the target of criticisms from people who do not practice structural analysis: "Your work is from the very start a vicious circle! You find as the end-product of your research nothing more than what you posited at the outset, and you involve yourself in a long search for what you have yourself hidden . . ." Indeed, any deductive method is open to such a criticism. Nevertheless, the analyst carries on his work, convinced as he is that the study of the systems and the classification of constants and variables is never useless.

As anyone can verify, when one sets aside the specific features which distinguish verbs from each other ("semantic restrictions") and again the subclasses from each other, all of them are reduced to *two classes*. These classes can be named after the two verbs which have the most general uses: "doing" and "being-having." This formulation presupposes that "having" is reducible, in most instances at least, to "being" (for instance, "having money" — "being rich;" "having an object" — "being the owner of it;" "having pain" — "being sick," etc.). Common language makes frequent use of the broad meaning of these verbs which could be termed "arch-predicates": "What did you do yesterday?" — "I worked, travelled, ate, played, cooked, etc." As Pascal would say, all this "is wrapped in the name of *action*." Similarly, for being-having: "What is it?" or "What is the matter?" — "I am tired, happy, surprised; I am afraid; I have a stone in my shoe; I have a bill to pay . . ." We call "*predicates*" the classes of *processes* which are determined in this way, in order to emphasize that we take into account only their syntactic function (and not the semantic constraints). We can therefore distinguish:

— the predicates of the class of "doing" = the *functions*

— the predicates of the class of "being" = the *qualifications*.

From now on these terms will have to be understood as defined above. We shall discuss the qualifications when dealing with the analysis of semantic contents (Chapter III). Let us consider the functions.

c) Classification of Functions

A quasi-total reduction led us directly to this fundamental crossroads where the analyst decides to consider one process as a function and another as a qualification. To deal efficiently and correctly with the class of functions and to uncover its organization, we must find an intermediary level. Such an intermediary level is characterized by a richer semantic investment and therefore by a narrower combinational possibility. At this level a few distinctions are established, and a few types (or subclasses) of functions present themselves as binary oppositions.

Usually, the following categories are taken into consideration.

Arrival vs. Departure
      Departure vs. Return: These functions are interrelated according to the category "movement" or "presence/absence."

Conjunction vs. Disjunction: Encounter of personages with other personages or their separation. Relation of spatial contiguity.

Mandating vs. Acceptance: (or vs. Refusal) An action is explicitly or implicitly proposed to an actor who accepts it or refuses it. . . . Interrelation according to the category "transitivity of the action or of volition."

Confrontation: (or Affrontment)	Presented in isolation as it is, this function raises special problems. Two actors confronting each other are exactly in symmetric positions. It could eventually be viewed as a binary opposition: Confrontation vs. Association (on the basis of the category Exclusion vs. Integration). We shall find this problem again when dealing with the "actantial" positions "helper/opponent."
Domination vs. Submission:	Victory vs. Defeat as end-product of the preceding function.
Communication vs. Reception:	Along the axis of the transmission (or transfer) of any kind of "objects."
Attribution vs. Deprivation:	This is another way to express the preceding function by opposing it to its negative form.

By means of the preceding list the processes can be reduced and classified. This list plays the role of the "grid" of crossword puzzles in which (as one knows in advance) all the words corresponding with the definitions can be written down. Indeed, a crossword puzzle is a deductive game and, yet, it is not without interest . . .

d) The Actantial Roles

As the processes can be reduced into functions/qualifications, so the *actors* (or personages) can be reduced into "actantial roles." For indeed, actors and processes are "isotopic" and vary practically in the same way. This is true even though their respective designation might seem to contradict this statement because these designations also account for the fact that their deep variation does not engender the same superficial variation. An example will clarify this point: "Peter got up, said good-bye, and went home." When reducing this sentence to the functions "disjunction" and "departure," one can keep the name of the actor: "Peter left." We could think that the reduction affected the process alone, while the actor Peter would remain equal to himself as if the human "subject" could keep his identity as an autonomous invariant through the vicissitudes of real life. But this is nothing but an illusion. This interpretation would misrepresent both the nature of literary personages and the interaction of actors and processes. A personage in a narrative is not constituted by a physical or psychical invariant but rather by a series of variations on a *syntactic invariant*. The illusion of a personage with a stable identity which is reinforced by the power of the proper name is nothing but a "narrative effect." This effect serves as a canopy for a subtle and artificial organization of variables completely dependent upon the total narrative interplay. Thus, the "Peter" of the process "Peter got up" is not quite identical with the "Peter" of the canonic statement, "Function: Departure" — Actant: Peter." The semantic weakening of the predicate led to the correlative weakening of the "subject" which is reduced to what is called an *"actantial role."* This is why in the formula of the canonic statement it is designated by A (for *actant*). In this perspective, the actor Peter looks like any other actor (e.g., John, Joseph, Mary) who occupies in another part of the narrative the same position as "subject" of the same predicate "going away." If it were not for a special mechanism which, as we shall see below, allows the registering and the summing up of the functional values ascribed fleetingly to the personages, the narrative would disintegrate into statements totally independent of each other. Once more, the goal of the analysis is the systematic reconstruction of the "crystals" of meaning formed in the narrative fabric. Consequently, the analysis does not consider the active "subjects" themselves but rather treats them as manifestations of a syntactical invariant. The only semantic investment of this invariant is made out of the variables which are the "classes of roles." The "classes of roles" are parallel with the "classes of functions."

We could have made the same observations about the actors which are in position of "direct object" or of "indirect object." "Peter gives Susan a bouquet." These three actors are three actantial roles organized around the function "communication-reception;" they are three "entities" which do not subsist by themselves in virtue of some physico-psychic "wholeness" but which receive their specific value from their simultaneous crossing of the space of the same statement.

A "personage" (and, as we shall see, "meaning" as a whole) is only a more or less ephemeral "flower" blooming on the narrative branch for the joy and edification of the reader. Of course, it is for the flower or the fruit that one takes patient care of the plant. Far from existing primarily for themselves, as real beings which are secondarily in relationship with each other, the actors of a narrative are above all in relationship with each other. The unstable "figures" created through this interrelationship are for them the sole horizon of existence. Consequently, as A. J. Greimas pointed out, the narrative statement in its simplest form can be defined by the formula F (A). Here, "function" (F) is to be understood in a quasi-mathematical sense.

We shall discuss below the complementary role of the "qualifications" in the formation of the personages.

e) The Residues after the Reduction

A reduction yields two results: a constant (which characterizes the class) and a number of variables (which are listed as "residues"). Yet, in a field as subtle as language what is a constant at the level of a class may be a variable when viewed in terms of a broader class and vice-versa. One should never destroy or permanently discard the "residues." They must be taken again into account at other stages of the analysis and to be integrated at a specific place of the semantic or stylistic system. In practice one learns quickly to distinguish and to recover these "residues" without the help of a huge written list. A semantic re-reading of a text previously analyzed in a syntactical perspective extracts quite easily those elements which had been neglected and considered as residues but which become now the prime objects of the analysis.

f) Modalities and Transformations

The interpretation of modalities and transformations is an essential and difficult stage of the analysis. Narrativity is, first of all, manipulation of modalities, exploitation of transformations: thus the importance of this part of the analysis. It is difficult because the linguistic presentation of the modalized statements can hinder the precise identification of the actantial roles and of the functions. We cannot deal in detail with this question which has been treated by A. J. Greimas (cf. specifically *Du Sens*, pp. 166-83), and by T. Todorov in his important article, "Les Transformations narratives" in the journal *Poétique*, 3, 1970, reprinted in *Poétique de la Prose*, Paris: Le Seuil, 1971, 225-40, and in *Dictionnaire Encyclopédique des Sciences du Langage*, Paris: Le Seuil, 1972, 368-74). In this essay we are focusing on the practice of narrative analysis: how to recognize and list modalized statements.

Let us take an example: "But the young archaeologist was not able to succeed in imagining her in the context of Rome, in this big city full of noise" (from *Délires et rêves dans "La Gravida" de Jensen*, text by Jensen and commentary by S. Freud).

Without difficulty we can apprehend a canonic statement behind the screen of the lexie. We can easily identify two actors: the "young archaeologist" (Norbert Hanold) and "her" (Gravida, a young lady represented on a Roman bas-relief that Norbert admired). But what is the "function"? Three verbs seem to be candidates for this designation: "being able," "succeeding," "imagining." Which one should we choose? What should we do with the two others? With the negation? The situation seems very complex. Yet, it could be even more confusing if the text had been,

"Norbert would have liked to be able to succeed in imagining that she did not live in Rome." The meaning would be almost the same and five verbs would be strung together. In order to put some order into the analysis, one needs to find the organizing principle of this complex. Once again the analyst has to identify the constants and the variables. We can use here the question suggested above: "What happens in the text?" or this other, "What is the basic statement around which the operators are organized?" or again, "If, in order to simplify the sentence, I take off successively each of the verbs which introduces another verb, directly or indirectly, which verb will remain at the end of the process?" It is clear that, in the first form of the sentence, all the verbs could be left aside because they are introduced by another one. "Being able" introduces "succeeding" which introduces "imagining" which has itself as object an implicit clause, "Gravida lives in Rome" or "Gravida is a young Roman lady." This construction appears more clearly in the transformed sentence, ". . . to imagine that she did not live in Rome." This latter formulation has the additional advantage of showing that the negation survived the disappearance of the verb to which it was attached, "being able." Nothing restrains us any longer from listing systematically the statement, even though the basic narrative statement will be more qualificative than functional (this is of little import here). We transcribe at the bottom the descriptive statement which represents the action or the situation in terms of which the operators of transformation intervene. They will figure in the formula as exponents.

Negation

      being able

           succeeding

               imagining

                    (DS:
                     S: Gravida
                     Q: Roman)
                     (=Gravida is
                     Roman)

("DS" for "descriptive statement;" "S" for "subject;" "Q" for "qualifier").

We can present it in another way:
NS1:F: to be able. A: Norbert. O: NS2. F: to succeed. A: Norbert.
O: NS3. F: to imagine. A: Norbert. O: DS. Q: Roman. S: Gravida.
("NS" for "narrative statement;" "F" for "function;" "A" for
"actor;" "O" for "object.")"

With such a formulation it is easier to see that the successive
statements are interrelated through explication of the *object*.
Norbert is able or not able to do something, and this "something"
is equal to "he succeeds to do something," etc.

Usually the texts do not present such a complex succession of
modalities. Hence, there is no reason to look at the modalities as
presenting a major difficulty. A few remarks about their
classification are in order. In the preceding example, the reader
will have noticed that the operation produced by the negation or
by the verb "to imagine" is not exactly the same as the operation
produced by the verb "to be able" or by the verb "to succeed." A. J.
Greimas keeps, for narrative analysis, *three main modalities*:
volition, power (being able to), cognition (*vouloir, pouvoir,
savoir*). We shall meet them again when discussing the relations in
the "actantial model." T. Todorov points out a larger number of
"*transformations*" of which the "modalities" are only peculiar
cases. According to Todorov, there are *six* "simple
transformations" (negation is one of them as transformation of
"status"; "succeeding" is another as transformation of "result").
There are also six "complex transformations" ("imagining" would
be an example as transformation of "*subjectivation*" or of
"knowledge").

It should be noted that this analysis of the modalities demands
at times the re-establishment of a complete descriptive statement
when the manifested text has suppressed the verb in order to
emphasize on the surface that this statement is playing the role of
object for the verbs of modality. This is what we found in our
example, "He was not able to succeed in imagining *her* . . ." It is
essential for the study of the narrative syntax that the basic
statement be reconstructed. We found earlier another example,
"Peter enjoys Paul's visit" is equivalent to "Paul visits Peter,"
transformed by an attitude. All this shows that the surface
syntactical roles (Peter is "subject," Paul is "a genitive") are

sometimes misleading insofar as what happens in a text is concerned. Yet, any locutor can find his way through this process on the basis of a common linguistic "competence."

g) The Different Types of "Doing"

As one progresses in the practice of structural analysis, more precise classifications and sharper tools for the analysis become necessary. Thus, the field of the "functions" (at the center of which is "doing") can be submitted to further structuring by taking into account the levels where "doing" can be located. A. J. Greimas distinguishes from among:

"*Somatic doing*" includes the physical relations such as "eating, moving, killing, receiving, stopping, travelling, picking up, being sick, attending, dying, healing . . . "

"*Communicative doing*" when the action is aimed at making known facts, events (which might eventually belong to the "somatic doing").

"*Interpretive doing*" when these events are reconstituted more or less subjectively on the basis of partial data and observations.

"*Persuasive doing*" when the activity is aimed at inducing a certitude in the minds of others . . .

All this would demand a detailed discussion. Yet a simple mention must suffice here. When these categories are needed in a specific analysis, we shall be in a position to come back to them on the basis of this first encounter. Thus, it appears clearly that the procedure presented here is neither complete nor exclusive. Practice shows that, after a first phase during which the concepts are applied in a wooden and mechanical way, the "analytical competence" includes the possibility of detecting new problems and adapting the methodology accordingly.

B. FROM STATEMENT TO CANONIC SYNTAGM

The title chosen for this second stage of narrative analysis suggests that there is a parallelism between the organization of the superficial elements in the sentence and that of the narrative elements in the discourse. Narrative statements are characterized by their ability to form a chain. They are not ordered haphazardly or according to the fancy of the narrator, but on the basis of predetermined relations, i.e., of a syntax or of a specific rule of combination. The functions follow one another according to a predetermined order, as words do in sentences. The results of such orderings are termed "*syntagms*" (a word which, like its cousin, *syntax*, evokes the arrangement in a single textual space). The syntagms are also "canonic" in that they are defined in terms of the system and not in terms of the performance. The relations which structure them remain constant behind the transformations provoked by the manifestations. Thus, it is always possible to make them reappear. This stage of the analysis is relatively easy if the construction of the canonic statement has been done correctly. The main canonic narrative syntagms have been progressively identified as a result of a great number of tentative analyses. The following syntagms are usually recognized:

The *contractual syntagms.* They are made out of *two functions* which are at once successive and symmetrical, mandating and accepting. One or the other may be implicit in the manifestation. They correspond to the *initial phase* of the narrative: an actor is invited, compelled, enabled by somebody (who may or may not be a personage) to perform a program of action. The *contract* is an essential element of a narrative. It is presupposed in any endeavor even if it is not explicitly mentioned. We shall come back to it when speaking of the actantial scheme. Let it suffice here to be able to recognize it as a syntagmatic element. Note also that it can take a negative form: the contract may be broken or it may never be established.

The disjunctional syntagms. They are made out of the successive *functions*: arrival and departure or departure and return. They are easy to identify and are a less determining factor in the structure of the narrative. But it is never useless to construct the "logic" and the correlations of the actors' *movements* and of their *encounters* with other actors. If it is true, as we suggested earlier, that personages receive an appearance of substance by crossing the narrative spaces, then their arrivals, their departures, and their presences with one or another actor are functional "limits" which structure both their identity and that of the other personages. We could even say that these functions define the "locus" of the narrative.

The *performancial syntagms.* They correspond to what A. J. Greimas often terms "tests" (*épreuves*). They are made from a succession of three statements:

NS1 = confrontation

NS2 = domination

NS3 = attribution.

The performancial syntagms represent a central point of transformation, a place of "decision" and of denouement. The two actors in opposition (subject and opponent, subject and anti-subject . . ., cf. below) are confronted by each other (NS1). One of the two opposite endeavors which characterize them must succeed, the other must fail (NS2). As a final result, the victorious actor receives an *object* (attribution) which will be used to fulfill a lack (NS3). Several performancial syntagms can be found in the same narrative and are characterized by different objects. What Vladimir Propp called "the villainy" (cf. V. Propp, *Morphology of the Folktale*, Austin: University of Texas Press, 2d edition, 1968, 30-35), belongs also to this type of syntagm.

Thus, statements can be included in superior hierarchic units. Once this is accepted, the question of the *actors* must be raised again. What happens to them in the syntagm? They are considered as *actants*. The concept of actant is more abstract and more general than that of "actantial role." It is borrowed from the linguist L. Tesnière (*Eléments de Syntaxe Structurale*, Paris, 1965). The systematic organization of the syntagms implies a narrower correlation (in terms of positions) of the actors. It becomes clearer that it is from each other that they receive their syntactic status, i.e., their position in the narrative fabric. The "natural" and holistic character of the personage is deconstructed and its relational truth appears.

In the *contractural syntagm* the ordered functions mandating + accepting presuppose a number of actantial roles which are both different and paradigmatically complementary, yet correlative and "reciprocal" (in a syntactically ordered reciprocity). The position of the mandating actant is logically prior to that of the accepting actant, which belongs to a different plane and presupposes the former. We have just defined to a first approximation two actantial positions, *sender* and *subject*.

In the *performancial syntagm*, the succession of functions reveals also a number of ordered actantial roles, *subject, opponent (or opposite subject)*, and *helper* which are implicit in the functions confrontation and domination. *Sender* and *receiver* correspond to the function attribution.

Here it is enough to understand that the *actant* as a class represents another level of invariants which represent the infinite number of actors (including all kinds of heroes and traitors). Such syntactic invariants correspond to spheres of correlative actions, to "poles of energy" ("*poles énergétiques*") and *not* to "types" of personages defined in terms of similarities in characters, i.e., in terms of non-analyzed "content effects."

Before going further, we deem it necessary to emphasize that the operation which allows the passage from the statement to the syntagm has a "residue": a number of semantic constraints which give to the personages the appearance of "full terms," i.e., of self-defined units. These semantic constraints are represented by the "actantial model" that we shall discuss together with the narrative sequence.

C. FROM SYNTAGM TO SEQUENCE

a) The Sequence

In the analytical procedure, a new step toward the construction of the discursive system is possible: several syntagms can be combined together into a larger unit, the *sequence*. At the level of manifestation, its "image" is at times altered, widened, or mutilated, yet the sequence determines in the narrative a number of interrelations which are often easy to apprehend. In the narrative grammar, the *sequence* is a syntactic macro-unit, an invariant defined by the relations among the syntagms. These are relations of implication and of presupposition. The syntagmatic succession which characterizes a narrative is the following:

— contractual syntagm
— disjunctional syntagm
— performancial syntagm

This set constitutes already a complete structure, i.e., a structure sufficient to generate a narrative either directly or by repetition according to various modalities in a succession of *sequences*. This latter possibility allows A. J. Greimas to account for the Russian folktales analyzed by V. Propp and which have *three tests*. Each of the three tests is different from the other only in that the nature of the communicated *object* is different:

Qualifying test for the communication of the *object-vigor*
Main test for the communication of the *object-value* or *goods*
Glorifying test for the communication of the *object-message*.

This type of succession of *sequences* follows a *syntagmic* model. It is noteworthy to find there also an *invariant*. One can perceive here how deeply A. J. Greimas transformed the results of V. Propp's analysis: from a syntagmatic and linear model we pass over to a model which can be interpreted paradigmatically. This is a decisive step in the narrative analysis.

In practice, the distinction among "qualifying," "main," and "glorifying" tests (which belong to corresponding sequences) is relative. We are not dealing with static and frozen states but with "effects of relations." What is a qualifying test at one level may be a main test at another level, etc. This is merely one of the consequences of the general principle of structural analysis formulated in linguistics by F. de Saussure: "Language is a system of differences." It is, as in the case of a specific number, for instance 12, which is designated as a "term" only because of an arbitrary decision for the sake of brevity, although this number could be referred to in terms of the rules of composition which generated it (6 x 2, 6 + 6, etc.). This observation about the sequence is valid at all the other levels of structural analysis.

b) The Actantial Scheme (or Model)

The actantial scheme (or model) is the next stage in the deconstructing of the personages. It reveals the complete network of relations in which the actants mentioned in connection with the syntagm are understandable. Behind each of the actors in a narrative there is a totally constraining "locus" of definitions, a matrix (in the mathematical sense of the term) which generates the discursive objects that we analyze. The actantial scheme as we describe it here has been elaborated by A. J. Greimas on the basis of the research of V. Propp and of E. Souriau (*Les 200,000 situations dramatiques*, Paris, 1950), in order to generalize very specific models. Each actantial position is defined by a group of relations to the other positions. Here is how Greimas presents it in its most general formulation:

$$\text{Sender} \longrightarrow \text{Object} \longrightarrow \text{Receiver}$$
$$\uparrow$$
$$\text{Helper} \longrightarrow \text{Subject} \longleftarrow \text{Opponent}$$

It includes *three axes*:

The *axis of communication*: *sender, object, receiver.* Along this axis lie all the phenomena of communication, transference, transmission, deprivation, lack, asking, virtual or real reception, etc. . . . It is on this axis that the object receives a first definition as "what is communicated, transmitted, missing, given back, asked for . . ." Yet one should not forget that the object lies also on a second axis and that it is therefore also defined in terms of its relation to the subject.

Identification of the position of sender is in many instances difficult because it is often implicit in the linguistic manifestation (the manifestation usually gives a privileged status to the subject). Nevertheless, the position of sender is always decisive in the analysis of the narrativity. It is necessary to learn how to recognize in the texts the indirect references to the position of sender. Often the "descriptions" represent it.

The *axis of volition: subject, object.* Upon this axis are the phenomena of *quest*, conquest, fight in order to acquire something, taking possession of what is first presented negatively as lack. The subject is almost exclusively defined along the axis of volition. It is the axis of the project and of the plot.

The relations between subject and object and between sender and object should not be confused. The subject does not perform the communication, nor is he characterized by the reception of the object. It may happen that, at the level of the manifestation, the subject and the receiver are manifested by the same personage. In such a case, the single personage occupies several actantial positions, each of which remains fully distinct at its own level. Thus at the *actantial* level the subject should not be confused with either the sender or the receiver. The subject cooperates in a decisive way in the communication, but in a subordinate way. He makes possible the transference by suppressing the obstacles which hinder communication, or by weakening the powers which had engendered deprivation. As an illustration of this role of the subject, consider the action of the "hero" in folktales. The hero does not act for himself but for a social order which needs to be restored because its very existence is threatened. The marriage which often concludes the adventure is an ulterior phase of the restoration (a glorifying test) distinct from the transmission of the *object-value.* This is even more true in texts which do not belong to the corpus of folktales. Greimas' method has the advantage of deeply re-interpreting these concepts so as to allow their use in the analysis of any narrative.

The object, defined earlier through its relation with the sender and the receiver, is now defined further through its relation with the subject. This characteristic sometimes facilitates the identification of the object. For, indeed, it is often hidden in the manifestation. At times it is difficult to know what is communicated. In such cases one looks for what is the aim of the "quest" of the subject, what the subject "wants," what is the field in which he is enabled to act.

The *axis of power: helper, subject, opponent.* "Power" is the second modality. One should not forget that it also serves to define the subject, which occupies the central position on this axis. "Power" (or sometimes "cognition," i.e., "know how") is indeed needed in order to pass from "volition" to action. Thus, there is room for the modality of "power" between the project (or plot) and the actualization. In some narratives, power is primarily manifested through the figures of the helper and of the opponent (which are in a way independent from "power" itself). Here I hesitate to use the term "personage," not only because the helper and the opponent are syntactic values, but also because in many instances they are represented not by anthropomorphic beings but rather by qualities of the hero or by inanimate objects (e.g., "magical objects"). The *opposing* force is nothing other than the "figuration" of the "negative power" of a second subject that Greimas also calls the *anti-subject* (cf. A. J. Greimas, *Du Sens. Essais sémiotiques.* Paris: Le Seuil, 1970, 172). This "inverse power" provokes deprivation, maintains lack, and hinders restitution up to the time when the lack is reduced by the helper.

Three questions still demand our attention.

a) In many narratives (with the exception of folktales), the actants "helper / opponent" are not manifested in figurative form. The analyst should not be misled. Any main test presupposes "power" and thus the communication in a prior qualifying test of a helper propositional to the difficulty of the main test. For, indeed, the confrontation of the two subjects (subject and anti-subject) takes place through the intermediary of "powers." This is a reminder that the personages are artificial constructs.

b) If the opponent is nothing more than the figuration of the inverse power of a symmetrical subject, it is because the actantial model should be viewed as twofold. A specific model in which the subject is characterized by the helper presupposes an anti-model in which the subject (an anti-subject) is characterized by the opponent. It is often useful to reconstitute as in a mirror this inverse model in which each of the actantial positions receives an inverse sign (one could say a "negative sign" but it is better to avoid at this point such a phrase which might prematurely imply a choice between good and evil . . .).

c) It is here that the question of the axiology of texts (or "systems of values") should be raised, as well as the question of the insertion of an "ideological" dimension. All of this complex problem cannot be discussed here.

D. CONCLUSIONS

With the presentation of the "actantial model" the description of the syntactical part of the analysis comes to an end. In concluding, we need to take inventory of what we have clarified and to discuss briefly some of the questions that we have left open (often simply by referring the reader to the indispensable works which treat more fully the theoretical basis for such an analysis).

a) The Paradigmatic Sequences

Some narratives have repeated sequences which belong not only to the syntagmatic model of the three tests, but also to a paradigmatic model: the interrelations of these sequences are of a paradigmatic type. By this we mean that the same actors have in repeated sequences the same actantial positions, or positions which vary correlatively and in an ordered way. It then becomes possible to form several series of sequences which are homologous even though they may be distant from each other and not syntagmatically related. This phenomenon has been discovered and studied by Francois Rastier in "Les niveaux d'ambiguité des structures narratives" (*Semiotica* III, 4, 1971). It is this article that one must study if the analysis of a text demands it.

b) Establishment of the Subject

Let us come back to more practical considerations. Assuming the methodological precision given above, I shall emphasize some textual features which need to be submitted to investigation at the beginning of the analysis.

Any action seems "natural." An actor kills somebody . . . another takes back by force or cunning a stolen object from somebody . . . someone is acknowledged as a hero or a traitor . . . in all this nothing surprises us, nothing invites us to make explicit the syntactic presuppositions. In the same way, in real life we often believe that we act on our own, that we are the sufficient source of our own actions. Yet, in structural analysis, any "natural effect" must be suspect. Its construction on the basis of a system of signs and of relations must be carefully investigated. Behind the "subject" of the process emphasized by the surface syntax, we must find *what establishes him in position of subject*, namely his relations to the sender, the object, the helper, and the opponent.

The relation of the subject to the sender demands further explanation. The presentation of the actantial scheme did not show the establishing of the subject. Yet a relation should be represented linking the sender with the subject for the communication of *volition*. One could also note that a similar relation between the two is the communication of *power* and eventually of *cognition* (that is, of the helper) from the sender to the subject. It is useful to understand why these two relations are not represented on the scheme by arrows linking the sender with the subject. It is because these are two peculiar cases of the overall communication registered on the axis sender-object-receiver. The modalities (volition, power, cognition) are objects of a communication, as any object, and the one who receives them is, first of all, a receiver. Yet, these are very special objects. Instead of maintaining the one who receives them as receiver, they establish him in a specific position (subject). This prior establishment of the subject is necessary in order to have an intermediary (the subject) which will facilitate the communication of the main object to the ultimate receiver. Thus, there is no incompatibility between the position of receiver and that of subject. Quite to the contrary — the subject is first a receiver. He can even become it again as receiver of the object-value itself: as is the case in love stories in which, incidentally, the desired object is also sender. In fact, very commonly the subject becomes again receiver in order to receive the object-message at the end of "glorifying test." These remarks should suffice to suggest the composite nature of the personages which gather together in themselves these various positions in the manifestation.

The reader will have noticed that it is around the object that this intersection of relations is found. Rarely does the text manifest this object very explicitly. Yet its place in the narrative must be determined. This is why we need to ask at the very beginning of the analysis, "What is lacked ? By whom? What is communicated? What are the objects which are transmitted? What are the 'loci' of communication?" If an object in the narrow and material sense of the term is communicated, we need to ponder what position it occupies or hides and to reconstitute the complete network of relations which lies under this "meaning effect." Here again, the "natural" should not mislead the analyst . . .

Note that the "negative" objects are manifested either as attribution of a "harmful" object, or as deprivation of a "useful" object. It is important at this stage to reconstruct the function of the "villainy" (according to Propp's terminology) which leads to the manifestation of the *lack* and definition of the *quest*. By means of this "villainy" it is possible to locate the *inverse* (or negative) sender who can, at that point, act without the intermediary of his helper. This helper of the negative sender will be the opponent of the positive subject, i.e., the hero (the negative subject being the traitor). This negative sender is often masked, unrecognizable. Indeed, this is often one of the characteristics of any sender. He may stay in the background and consequently not be represented in the manifestation in any specific way (the society or one of its aspects occupies frequently the position of sender . . .).

c) Syntactic vs. Semantic

In concluding this first part, we can now go back to an important point that we had promised to discuss further, the distinction between *syntactic order* and *semantic order* in narrativity. The semantic elements more or less mask the emptiness of the syntactic elements and their indifference toward meaning. It is to the semantic elements that we have ascribed the "meaning effects" or, better, the "content effects." These effects are produced in the manifestation by a power which progressively narrows the otherwise open syntactic "possibilities." This is to say that, at first glance at least, there is the same opposition between syntactic and semantic as exists between "container" and "content" (their reciprocal heterogeneity and exteriority being included in this opposition). We could be tempted to think that the only value to the knowledge of the syntactic "container" would be that it would allow better identification of the content viewed as the only valid end of the analysis. Yet, we should not forget that this filling up with contents is necessarily closely interrelated with the progressive interplay of the syntactic forms. In other words, the "container" is not given a priori. It emerges in the text and its organization is the result of specific operations which belong to the syntactic process. Thus we cannot merely attribute the content effect to the crystallization of the external semantic values. Both the syntactic and the semantic orders contribute to producing the meaning effect. We shall discuss below how we can apprehend the interplay of these complementary orders.

On several of the topic discussed above, see the informative discussion in Philippe Hamon's articles:

"Pour un statut sémiologique du personnage," in *Littérature* 6, May 1972, 85-110.

"Analyse du récit," in *Le Français Moderne* 3, July 1972.

"Qu'est-ce qu'une description?" in *Poétique* 12, 1972, 466-85.

Chapter III

Analysis of Semantic Contents

Even though it involves a quite different procedure as compared with the syntactic analysis described above, semantic analysis is nevertheless a structural analysis in that it aims at uncovering the relational nature of the signifying constructs. It is essential in that it leads to the understanding of this superior effect of the text which is commonly called "meaning" or "signification" and which could be more precisely referred to as the "*signified*."

It seems "natural" that a discourse be uttered in order to have meaning. For us, this seems to be a self-evident truth (and thus one impossible to analyze). As trees bear fruit or plants give flowers, discourses produce meaning. We must glean the meaning in the same way as the businessman must glean a profit from his deals. This feeling is reinforced by the quasi-impossibility of producing utterances without any meaning, except when reading the letters of the alphabet for an ophthalmologist, or when singing a melody using meaningless phonemes because we have forgotten the words . . . or again when repeating without concern for the meaning a few phrases of a foreign language that we shall have great difficulty remembering because, "when you don't know the meaning . . ." Jacques Lacan, from a quite different perspective, emphasizes how easily the pure signifier remains unnoticed even and mainly when it is exposed in the forefront of our discourses. In such cases it slips out of the conscious, where it does not have any room, into the subconscious, as in the case of *The Purloined Letter* which was simultaneously exposed to sight and relegated to oblivion because of the signified which covered it as with a veil (cf. Jacques Lacan, *The Purloined Letter*, Yale French Studies, 1973). We should not be surprised by this phenomenon. In the actual use of discourse, as well as in reading, we are accustomed to manipulating meaningful units, the words of the syntagms that we find immediately available in our lexicon are already semanticized. It is not the quasi-mechanical use of the sentential syntactic rules which could reveal to us the frequent and subtle changes in the elementary meanings of each word (what we call sometimes the "proper" sense, or the "strict" sense, or again the "narrow" sense . . .). When we do not take time to reflect upon it we are very close to imagining that the process through which meaning is formed is nothing but a quantitative addition. Are not the words added one after another? Similarly, we have commonly a linear, additive understanding of meaning in the discourse or the narrative. Such a representation assumes that the syntactic and the semantic are heterogeneous and exterior to each other. It is on this point that we must begin to raise questions. Is not the artificial hidden behind the natural, the construct behind the meaning?

It is easy to observe that the interplay of meaning in a sentence is not the mere addition of the basic significations of the various terms. As Greimas shows in his *Sémantique structurale*, the meaning of a sentence proceeds by *constructing semic figures* which are more or less unstable and more or less foreseeable. These semic figures that Greimas termed *sememes* are *syntagmatic configurations of semes*. They are syntagmatic in that they can exist only at the level of the syntagm. *Seme* is a term which designates the minimal unit of the signified and is borrowed by Greimas from Bernard Pottier's important works on semantics (cf. Bernard Pottier, "Vers une sémantique moderne," *Travaux de linguistique et de littérature*, 1964, 107-38). Either semes are said to be "nuclear" when they participate in the semantic invariant (Pierre Guiraud calls the nuclear semes, "significations"). Or, the semes are said to be contextual either in the sense that they are redundant semes common to several lexemes of the context, or in the sense of free semes (also called classemes) which insure a regulation and a homogenization of meaning. These phenomena, although difficult to register with precision, are essential because they lead, in Greimas' theory to the notion of construct semes (to be discussed later). This is how one can explain the formation of the various meanings of the word "head" in the various syntagms: man's head, head of cattle, bridgehead, head of line, headline, letterhead, headwaiter, head water, etc.

This brief excursus was necessary in order to help us understand that the surface effect of the discourse (which seems to be the properly human feature and the ultimate expression of our "linguistic performance") is the manifestation of a process of construction. This process can be analyzed and deconstructed. Yet we are still at the level of the syntagm and the sentence. The study of the narrative phenomena raises this problem at the level of the larger configurations mentioned above. What about the semantic content of the narrative as a whole? Are we not aware of its charm and homogeneity? Are there constructions which are purely discursive and which could produce meaning effects impossible to reduce either to lexical significations (i.e., to various senses of terms in narrow and frozen contexts) or to significations produced in the free syntagms and in the sentences? Can we envision, beyond the sememes of a first level, a new class that we could call, following Greimas, "construct sememes?"

A. INTERPLAY OF MEANING
IN SYNTACTIC COMBINATIONS

We need to return to the problem of the relationship of the syntactic with semantic components. We need to understand why, indeed, meaning can only appear as the result of a twofold ordered process which organizes what we could eventually call the *condensation* (semantic aspect) and the *distribution* (syntactic aspect). If it were not for a representation of this type (whatever might be the reservations or the modifications that it deserves . . .) what would have been the purpose of scrutinizing so meticulously the syntactic framework? If one would have to conclude that the discourse does not manipulate the semantic units in any other way than the sentence (this would amount to saying that the sole pertinent syntax is the syntax of the sentence . . .), the analysis of the contents could be carried out without difficulty on the basis of a lexematic listing and of a relatively easy organization of the words which are most obviously semantized (for instance, all the qualifying terms and syntagms). To push this reasoning to the limit, one could then admit that the semantic content of a general and abstract sentence could be the equivalent of a whole novel. A good philosophico-moralistic commentary could take the place of all the narratives of the world! But we have shown that narrativity operates on the basis of both the actantial scheme and the configurations of the canonic functions, a kind of "distribution" of the roles which commands the distribution of the "figures" of the meaning.

In simpler terms let us attempt to envision the consequences, for the formation of meaning effects, of the fact that a given semantic feature is ascribed to a specific position in the actantial or functional scheme. Since all the positions of these schemes are correlated with each other, it is easy to understand that such an ascription would have immediate repercussion on all the other positions according to an interplay of constraints easy to reconstruct. This phenomenon corresponds, at the level of the sentence, to this other well-known phenomenon of the relative compatibility/incompatibility of grammatical subjects and verbs: "The fisherman catches a fish/the fisherman hunts a tree." This immediate repercussion (or diffraction) of the semantic restrictions in the syntactic network leads to a fragmentation of meaning which allows for a multiplication, a redundancy, a "sparklingness" of the manifestation and, thus, for a manifestation richer in semantic content. One could speak metaphorically of a semantization by capillarity or envision the behavior of meaning as similar to that of the ink on an ink-blotter or, again, as similar to a gas which occupies all the available volume . . . It has long been recognized that it is impossible to locate the meaning of a sentence in one or another of its lexemes. This phenomenon is now expanded to the dimension of the discourse or even of the text.

What are the consequences for the analysis? The actantial positions and the intersections of the functions are like many mirrors which reflect the figures of meaning with all the possible interplays of reproduction, complementation, inversion, superposition . . . Consequently, one can enter into the meaning through several doors (actantial positions or canonic functions). Yet it is necessary to know, at all times, how the figures of meaning are reflected by the complete set of mirrors and where to find the point of the reading within the choreography which involves all the actors — here compared to dancers in a ballet. Whether from inside the text or sometimes from outside, the locus of what controls and determines meaning is the intersection between the necessity demanded for the emergence of meaning and the infinite variety allowed by the system. This point of control, termed *axiology* or system of values, or even "ideology," allows evaluation of the movement and the exchange of elements of meaning. As some say, "anaphora and difference" are the two necessary principles in the discourse for the manifestation of meaning.

At any rate, the analyst has a great number of possibilities available for identifying the contents of the text. The same semantic element can take simultaneously the most varied forms as it is ascribed the positions of sender, object, receiver, subject, helper, or opponent, and even the symmetrical positions of the inverse model. Consequently, in order to apprehend any semantic element in all its rich complexity, one needs to enter into the interplay of meaning. Even the "functions," on the basis of their elementary form, must obey the demands of this *isotopy* of the global manifestation. All this creates an effect of coherence that we recognize spontaneously as characteristic of meaning. Such a coherence can take various forms and be established despite the presence of more or less stubborn incoherencies.

Finally, by taking into account the interplay of meaning in the syntactic combinations we can distinguish between what Greimas calls *inverse* forms and *posited* forms of the content as they are found at the beginning or at the end of the narrative, respectively. Further, the distinction between *topical content* and *correlated content* can be similarly understood as another phenomenon of diffraction of the meaning at one or another point in the text. It is now possible to understand also why these symmetrical semantic contents take a form which is both broken/reestablished *contract* and interrupted/restored *communication*: the syntactic form of contract-communication is self-semanticized and becomes one of the first figures of meaning.

The distinction between two types of predicates has been established above as corresponding to the two types of statements, doing vs. being. Narrative analysis has given a privileged place to the functions. Now, we need to emphasize that the passage from one type to the other (which is always possible) represents another aspect of the semantic dimension of the narrativity. We have seen that most adjectives are equivalent to functional paraphrases. "He spends much = he is rich"; "he gives all that he has = he is generous"; "He talks a lot = he is talkative"; etc. An analogous phenomenon happens in discourse; the functions performed by the actors are not merely transitory data about the development of the adventure and the fate of personages. The semantic content of these functions is put to the credit of the actors. The actor is first an empty ledger on the top of which is written only a proper name. As the narrative progresses, this empty ledger is progressively filled up with the entries (virtual qualifications) implied in the functions, and the personage is progressively created (the "hero" and the "traitor" being the personages who receive the greatest number of entries). From time to time, the text adds up these credits and debits and shows the present status of each of the personages in the form of explicit qualifications (either positive or negative). At any stage of its development the narrative is an up-to-date ledger, although it may delay the disclosure of the actual state of a personage's "account." This allows for special effects; the narrative conceals the actual nature of the personage behind ambiguous and even misleading appearances. Thus, although the narrative defines the personage as it unfolds itself, there is in the text an interplay of secret and manifestation, of lie and truth, up to the final revelation of the true content which is communicated.

The relationship between the qualifications as qualifying predicates and the "qualification" of the subject in the first test will be dealt with elsewhere. Let us note simply that, despite a close relationship, these two types of qualifications are nevertheless quite distinct in that they present different phases of the conversion of functions into qualifications. The art of narrating demands that specific functions be not immediately converted into qualifications, ie., into contents which at once define and establish the personage's value. In this way the narrative may keep its dynamism. A kind of equilibrium is maintained between movement and stability, succession and permanence — that is to say, between syntagm and paradigm.

C. PERSONAGES AND LOCATIONS

Often, locations have the same behavior as personages in narratives. Both are centers of crystallization which start as empty forms (proper names) and are progressively filled up with semantic features. In this way, they remain in the reader's memory as dependable and well known landmarks. They serve as invariants of the performance, loci in which are registered the variables which pass through the narrative space. They are familiar subjects and objects with which the reader establishes quasi-real relationships.

In his book, *Sémiotique de la Passion. Topiques et figures* (Coll. B. S. R. Aubier Montaigne, Paris: Cerf, 1971) Louis Marin provides excellent examples of how personages and locations are centers of crystallization in the narrative.

D. FROM SUPERFICIAL CONTENT
TO DEEP CONTENT

Greimas' theory of narrativity includes the distinction between the deep level and the superficial level (i.e., the level described above which should not be confused with the level of the manifestation or surface level). While the deep level is purely "logical," the superficial level is "anthropomorphic" (cf. the actants). Thus, beyond the laws which govern the figuration, the spatial localization, and the temporal succession, there would be a non-anthropomorphized state of the contents. At this deep level, the terms are determined and ordered by strictly logical laws and operations. They are then described in terms of the "semiotic square" which is closely related to the "logical square" or "logical hexagon." Here, it is enough to refer the reader to R. Blanché, *Les structures intellectuelles*, Paris, 1966.

This deep level is reached by the analysis at the ultimate stage of the deconstruction of personages, locations, and objects. Then the functions which had been previously identified as confrontation, domination, attribution are translated in logical terms as contradictory, contrary, affirmation, negation, implication. On this, see A. J. Greimas, "The Interactions of Semiotic Constraints," *Yale French Studies*, 1968.

Let us emphasize simply that at this deep level we find the ultimate and radical conversion of the functions into qualifications. Thus, narrativity would be the manifestation of an achronic and nonspatial manipulation of semantic contents which are interrelated in fundamental categories of the signification. This theory of an achronic basis of the narrativity raises numerous and difficult problems, yet it also explains quite a few phenomena (for instance, why narratives can be used in philosophical discourses).

CONCLUSIONS

Narrative Statement and Enunciation

In the preceding pages I have attempted to recast the various elements of a theory of one type of structural analysis into a procedural model. In so doing I took the risk of committing some errors. This is why these methodological elements should be submitted to a twofold control. They must be fleshed out by the reading of the basic works (and especially A. J. Greimas, *Sémantique structurale* and *Du sens*). They must also be controlled through the actual practice of structural analysis of narrative: we have proposed a *construct* model which must remain open to modification. Furthermore, our presentation is unilateral; we have focused all our attention on the *statement* and the meaning *produced*. This was necessary for the coherence of our presentation and also because of its procedural character. These pages are an attempt to enter the problematic determined by scholars involved in structural analysis of narrative, in order to establish the basic elements of our own method as well as to evaluate the problems involved in such an endeavor. It is this first methodological approximation that we shall have to readjust. Our doubts will have to be taken into account; the preceding pages are not to be viewed as an absolute method which should be applied mechanically. Quite to the contrary, recognizing the aim and the presuppositions of the original method, we are invited to build upon it and to use it creatively. It is when we believe that we must abandon this or that aspect of a given procedure that we are to be most grateful to the method which inspired this procedure: it allowed us to progress.

The emphasis put on *statement* in the preceding pages is not innocent. First, it led us to dismiss by economy almost entirely the dimension of enunciation. This was not meant to imply that enunciation is to be left aside as unimportant. Second, it led us to an analysis which is of a *logical* type (at the level of the narrative and not of the sentence) by presupposing a system in the statement (as a product of enunciation). This can engender a false representation which needs to be carefully avoided. We could indeed be led to believe that there would be a substratum which could not be analyzed and which would be the substantial foundation of the relations. This would lead us back into the unfortunate distinction between form and content (which has nothing to do with Hjelmslev's categories). What benefit would there be to conceive of a *primary meaning* preexisting in an ideal universe, without form and groping for a means of expression? Greimas' method, when exposed and used by Greimas himself or by his best disciples, avoids all these pitfalls. In fact, there is no "Greimas-orthodoxy" but an openness to revision of the theory.

This type of analysis must be complemented by research on the problem of *enunciation*, that is, of the *production* of the text. This is the condition necessary to maintain the relational aspect at each of the levels of analysis. This conclusion has been written in order to make room for such a reflection on enunciation, although work in this field is just beginning. One day, perhaps, the theory will be re-oriented by the inventory and the analytical study of the conditions of the production of the text (which is linguistically reproduced in the "enunciation notations" which represent in images the "little drama of the enunciation.") This would eventually lead to changing part of the procedure. But, of course, this will take time and thoughtful reflection. Yet, we do not expect that these new perspectives will lead to a dismissal of the above analytical procedure of statement as a whole. It will, rather, sharpen it.

On the question of enunciation, there are already a few published works. See especially Emile Benveniste's work, *Problèmes de linguistique générale*, Paris, 1966; English translation, *Problems in General Linguistics*, Miami Linguistic Series 8, Coral Gables, Florida: University of Miami, 1971. Benveniste appears more and more as a precursor. See also the essays by T. Todorov and O. Ducrot in *Dictionnaire Encyclopédique des Sciences du Langage*, and the works of M. Pécheux: his essay in *Langages* 24 and his book, *Analyse automatique du discours*, Dunod, 1969.

Part II

Temptation of Jesus in the Wilderness

Structural Analysis of a Narrative

Introduction

The following essay is defined by its relationship to two other texts:

— The preceding presentation of the procedures for a structural analysis of narrative derived from A. J. Greimas' method. The following analysis is an application of these procedures which does not pretend to be more than a sample or an exercise.

— The chapter dealing with the temptation of Jesus in Louis Marin's book *Sémiotique de la Passion* (Chapter II, 111-23). We fully accept the conclusions of this excellent analysis. Thus, we do not intend to correct it nor to complement it but, rather, to explicate some of the analytical procedures. For this purpose we need first to follow the Gospel text step by step in order to note and elicit all the relations and then to organize them into a coherent system. This approach is demanded by the method which we have chosen. Consequently, our presentation might appear to be less dependent upon Marin's work than it really is. This impression is reinforced by the fact that Louis Marin uses a method which is derived not only from Greimas' semiolinguistic theory but also from Jacques Lacan's understanding of the relations between *signifier* and *subject* — the second part of Marin's book, *La sémiotique du traître*, is introduced by a quotation from Lacan. It is only in this light that it can be fully understood. Our own explanation is almost exclusively focused upon the semio-linguistic procedures. Thus, in a longer essay, we shall present less "content."

We shall analyze the temptation story found in Matthew 4:1-11 in the translation of *The Jerusalem Bible*. At times we shall show how our text is related to the text of Luke 4:1-13 and other pericopes of the Gospels. Such discussions are not part of literary critical methods, nor are they an attempt to write a "history of the composition" of our text. Rather, these comparisons are made so as either to verify or complement our study of a system of signification. Our appeal to the Greek text, when useful, will be justified and explained. But it must not constitute an excuse to avoid the problems raised by the analysis of the chosen version.

Chapter I

Narrative Structures of the Temptation Story

At the outset of our analysis we have a readable Gospel text which can be divided into lexies. The first step of our procedure attempts to uncover the ordered network of relations governing the combination of meaningful units and imposing constraints upon the interplay of meaning. More specifically, this first analysis aims at constructing a functional and actantial model of the text. This model is a syntactic system which is responsible for generating the narrative on the basis of semantic invariants to be analyzed in the following chapter. Thus, from the sentences or linguistic statements we progressively construct this model of the syntactic system: a system represented by the *functions*, the *syntagms*, and the *sequences*, and by the *actantial roles, actants*, and *actantial model*.

As a whole, these analytical operations represent a kind of mathematical reduction of the text which should result in a classification of the constants and variables. If there are "residues," as we can expect from such operations, we shall take note of them in order to analyze them as semantic values in the following chapter.

Lexie 1
Then Jesus was led by the Spirit out into the wilderness to be tempted by the devil.

First, we take note of the actors or personages which in this case are explicitly named: Jesus, the Spirit, and the devil. Similarly, we list the processes manifested by the verbs which express, as nearly as they can be expressed on the textual surface, the relations among the actors: "was led out into the wilderness, to be tempted." These processes hide in their depths the functions. A relation is also hidden in the lexeme "to." From the perspective of a grammatical analysis, we could say that "to" expresses purpose.

49

We shall see below how it can be analyzed in a structural perspective. We have listed "into the wilderness" as a mere qualification of the process "to lead." The wilderness is not an actor but a location, and its relation to other elements of the lexie is not of the same type as the relations we have noted among the actors. The actors are related two by two. The wilderness is related to the three actors and it does not represent a function.

Without changing the lexie significantly we can transpose the passive form of the two processes into their active form. "The Spirit led Jesus out into the wilderness" so that "the devil might tempt him." This transposition is always useful and possible: the passive sentence is the transformed form of the corresponding active sentence. Such a transformation does not alter the meaning significantly, as the proponents of generative and transformational grammars have shown.

It is now possible to pass to the level of the canonic statements in which the functions and the actantial roles can be discussed. On the basis of the active form, "the Spirit led Jesus out into the wilderness," we can recognize two subordinated statements:

1) "Jesus goes into the wilderness," a statement of movement. There is an implicit function, *departure*, and an explicit function, *arrival*. These two functions are intransitive: the subject is set in relation to himself. This is well expressed by the reflexive form (middle voice). Jesus plays here, so to speak, two actantial roles, subject and object.

2) The Spirit does something to Jesus. It makes Jesus perform the movement. This is a contractual statement with its twofold functions, *mandating* and *acceptance*, which are manifested here in a syncretistic way. We could also say that this is a statement of communication of volition. The Spirit is in the actantial position of sender, Jesus in that of receiver who is invested with the position of subject by this mandating. It clearly appears that the sender is the one who assigns the roles in a narrative.

The rest of the sentence needs to be analyzed in two steps:

1) "The devil will tempt (or is going to tempt) Jesus." We need to identify the function manifested in the verb "to tempt." Taking

into account the rest of our text, we can transpose this phrase into another in which the narrative elements are more clearly manifested: "the devil will propose to Jesus to do something." We can then easily identify structural elements similar to those we found in the first part of the lexie:

— A narrative statement of "doing" with Jesus invested as potential subject. It could also be termed a modal narrative statement of *hypothetical* volition (i.e., a program of action with indetermination as an additional modality). "Jesus is susceptible of willing to do something."

— A statement of communication of volition. The devil is the sender of this volition and Jesus the potential receiver. It is interesting to note the parallelism between the actantial role of the Spirit and that of the devil. We shall come back to it.

Jesus is thus established in a complex role: he is invested with the volition communicated earlier by the Spirit, and he is the one to whom another volition communicated by the devil will be proposed. Thus, the text manifests its most characteristic feature in its first sentence: a twofold investment of the actantial position of sender. The object to be communicated (i.e., the program which these volitions define) is not yet specified. In the first narrative statement (where the Spirit is sender), the determination of the object is found only in the statement of movement which actualizes it. Yet, it might be possible to see a relationship between this partial contract and the general contract manifested in the baptism story immediately preceding our text. More specific observations shall further suggest the interrelation of these two texts. In the second narrative statement (where the devil is sender), the object does not receive any other determination than the semantic content of the predicate "to tempt," which represents a "quotation" from a rich cultural code. Here, it is enough to register it as the proposal of a contract opposed to the first contract. Pursuing our examination of the intratextual correlations, this second program proposed to Jesus is made explicit in the subsequent functions.

2) What is the relationship between the two pairs of statements

linked by ". . . to . . .?" It is at least a spatio-temporal relationship: "The Spirit led Jesus out into the wilderness, *then* and *there* the devil is going to tempt him." There is also a relationship of order or of logical priority: Jesus must first go into the wilderness before being tempted. This brings about a certain disequilibrium in the symmetry of the two positions of sender. The devil can assign roles only in a "second time" (after an initial manifestation of the Spirit). The devil's position as tempter presupposes a specific location to which Jesus, led by another, must go. It is to be noted that the passive form, "to be tempted by the devil," weakens the correlation between the Spirit and the devil and consequently emphasizes that their only point in common is Jesus. Thus, the personage, Jesus, appears as a mediator, i.e., as the "intersection" of two narrative spaces or sets in which can be apprehended the subtle correlation of two unequal and yet symmetrical senders. However, this remark belongs to the semantic analysis and is, therefore, premature. It is always a temptation to reintroduce too early in the discussion the residues of the functional analysis (e.g., the value of the terms "to be led," "to tempt," and "wilderness"). We should simply keep them in mind.

A quick study of both the Lukan text and the Greek text shows that the syntactic structure is identical. We find the same actors, the same functions. The only difference is a more discreet manifestation of the correlation between the two pairs of statements: Luke 4:1-2, "Jesus . . . was led by the Spirit through the wilderness, being tempted there by the devil for forty days." The Greek text of Matthew expresses this correlation by using a simple aorist infinitive.

Lexie 2

He fasted for forty days and forty nights, after which he was (very) hungry.

We may say first that the two processes — those of fasting and being hungry — are strictly intransitive. This is confirmed by the fact that only one actor is manifested, Jesus. Yet when we look to the functions, we note that fasting is the negative transformation of eating, i.e., doing what must be done in order to ingest food. Being hungry is the stylistic transformation of needing food (thus being in lack of something). From the perspective of the narrative analysis, we can apprehend two transformed canonic statements:

1) "Fasting:" a descriptive narrative statement. There is no confrontation capable of achieving the transmission of the object. We could say that this is a "non-test" (in the narrative sense of the term). Thus, the subject Jesus does not carry out the performance necessary for the communication of the object-food.

More specifically, what is the structure of this statement? It is one of the three (NS1, NS2, NS3) performancial statements. Therefore it should manifest at least *two* actantial positions, subject and opponent (or anti-subject). Against what or against whom must one struggle in order that food might be communicated? Furthermore, who will be the sender of the food at the end of the performance (cf. statement of attribution: NS3)? These points are not explicated by the text, they are presupposed. Everybody knows that (a)"eating" admits of an action and thus belongs to the opposition "action vs. passivity"; and that (b) without contributions from nature and society man cannot expect to have any food. The negation of these values in the process "fasting" already suggests elements of the meaning of the text. The semantic analysis will have to take these elements into account.

2) "Being hungry:" a descriptive narrative statement (NS3 of the performance). It expresses the non-communication of the object, food. The sender X does not communicate food to the receiver Jesus. It is the direct consequence of the absence of a test. As a result, we find the *situation of lack* (which characterizes the beginning of a narrative in V. Propp's perspective). We can observe that the lexematic manifestation of the structure is not fully adequate: "after which he was hungry." Of course, hunger must have occurred before forty days had gone by! But it is enough for the text to manifest the pertinent functions which draw attention to the intervention of the second sender, even though this remark will be valid only for the first temptation.

Lexie 3
And the tempter came and said to him . . .

In this scene we have two actors, the tempter and Jesus. Two processes manifest the relations established between them, "came" and "said to him" (the object of "saying" will be dealt with in the following lexie). The first process involves a single actor, "the devil moves." This process has "he is near Jesus" as a consequence. The second process includes two actors and an object (message). The canonic statements can easily be apprehended.

1) "The tempter came:" a descriptive narrative statement, function — movement, subject — the tempter. This movement is in some ways correlative with what Jesus accomplishes when coming into the wilderness. This representation confers upon the devil the appearance of an anti-subject (or traitor) who confronts the hero in the main combat, but this is in fact an earlier phase of the narrative structure. Indeed, in addition to the movement, we find the conjunction of the two personages ("he is near Jesus") but they are joined together for a communication and not for an overt struggle. The text presents the movement of the messenger and his conjunction with the potential receiver. This statement belongs to the contractual stage of the narrative structure.

2) "And said to him:" a descriptive narrative statement, function — communication, sender — Satan, receiver — Jesus, object — message. The devil remains a potential sender who would assign the roles. The object that he proposes is a message. What does it involve? It is too early to tell, but the rest of our text will explain it.

Lexie 4
If you are the Son of God, tell these stones to turn into loaves.

This statement manifests the object of the communication. It includes three processes related to one another through a subtle hierarchy.

"Jesus is the Son of God." This is not, strictly speaking, a process. We should not look for a function here but, rather, for a qualification. Nevertheless, a relation is established between Jesus as interlocutor of the devil ("you") and the qualification, "Son of God."

"Jesus gives an order." This is an actual process, a "performancial" word. Jesus accomplishes something by speaking.

"The stones turn into loaves." A process of transformation.

What are the exact relations among these various processes? The surface grammar presents a conditional clause ("*If* you are . . .") and a consecutive clause ("then do . . . and these stones will become loaves"). But what are the canonic statements?

Confronted with complex manifestations, we can make two hypotheses. On the one hand, it is possible that we are in the presence of a basic statement modified by several operators or several modalities, yet on the other hand, it is also possible that the manifestation anticipates the potential syntagmatic unfolding of the functions. It is this second possibility which accounts for our lexie. In his proposition, the devil suggests both the program of action that Jesus is capable of performing ("would you turn these stones into loaves?") and also a summary of the tests and their consequences which the sender's proposal places before the potential hero. This brief sentence of our text is to be viewed as a mirror in which a *possible* narrative is reflected — i.e., what would happen, from A to Z, if Jesus would accept the devil's proposition? In such a case, the statements would be organized as follows:

1) *Main test* with its three statements:

NS1.   Function — confrontation,   subject — Jesus, opponent — the nature of things, helper — the Word. Jesus is confronted with natural reality in which stones are stones and not loaves. In order to overcome this obstacle, he must make use of a power which will be able to modify this order so that loaves might appear where stones had been. The devil suggests that he should use his "word:" "tell . . . " (εἰπέ). The devil implies that Jesus' word is adequate for this task. This presupposes a qualifying test that we shall discuss below.

NS2.   Function — domination,   subject — Jesus, opponent — the nature of things, helper — the Word. Insofar as the word of Jesus is viewed as the power which enables the subject to neutralize the obstacle, the test will be positive: the stones will become loaves. In this statement we are even further away from the real order than in NS1, and the argument is even more clearly hypothetical.

NS3. Function — attribution, sender — X, receiver — Jesus, object — loaves. Thus, in terms of manifestation, Jesus obtains loaves. His need for food can be satisfied. The *lack* is remedied. This is the conclusion of the main test. Here again, we have to take into account the implicit character of this statement and its twofold modalization (in terms of the hypothetical future). The manifestation is very condensed and elliptical.

The detailed reconstruction of the statement shows the precise value of the two terms, stones and loaves. The first is presented as real, present, already here. "These stones . . ." are an element of the concrete situation which by metonymy can ultimately represent any natural element — i.e., any element which is entirely defined by the network of natural laws and relations (and therefore excludes any definition in terms of its relations with men). It is what is given by nature, a primary order. This natural condition and constraint delimit the condition and liberty of man. These stones must be replaced by the loaves which are characterized by all of the opposite signs. They are absent as long as the stones are here. They are meant for man, defined as they are by the possible usage that man can make of them. They will be ($\gamma\acute{\epsilon}\nu\omega\nu\tau\alpha\iota$) here in place of the stones. They will be signs of an order reconstructed around man, by him and for him. By transforming the stones into loaves, Jesus is invited to substitute himself for the order of nature and to become somehow his own sender (which we have noted above as sender — X) in the same way that man does. For, indeed, man is able to provide for his own subsistence by his work better than nature can. What is different with Jesus is that his intervention would be entirely independent of the natural constraints. We shall have the occasion to verify and eventually to specify this analysis below. The narrative system begins to take shape and it remains for us to include in it other elements of the text.

2) *Qualifying test.* The attribution of the *helper.*

We have noted that the obstacle to the communication of the object-value must be overcome in the main test by an adequate *power* of the hero (object-vigor). The verb *tell* suggests that this power is here related to the "word." The question of its attribution to the hero during a qualifying test must be raised. Without any doubt, the mention of the divine sonship (in the conditional clause, "If you are the Son of God . . . ") represents the very source of the hero's qualifications and therefore the "locus" from which the helper is obtained. It is because he is (or, in the devil's perspective, because he presents himself as) Son of God that Jesus can count upon a creative or transforming word. Thus, the phrase, "Son of God" implies both the gift of the helper and also the *contract* which invests Jesus in the actantial role of subject. The story of the Baptism is without any doubt presupposed in the tempter's proposition.

3) Glorifying test. The acknowledgment of the hero.

Although less explicitly so than with the two other tests, the third one is suggested and hidden by the same formula, "If you are the Son of God." In fact, the mark of the glorifying test characterizes the whole adventure which is proposed to Jesus and still remains a significant factor after the completion of the first two tests. It could be formulated as follows: " . . . tell these stones to turn into loaves, and it will be clear that you are the Son of God." Thus, the program proposed by Satan includes the acknowledgment of Jesus as sent by the Father. This glorifying acknowledgment would occur as the consequence of a manifestation of Jesus' power which is capable of transforming the human condition for his own benefit.

Such a narrative framework could eventually account satisfactorily for the first temptation. The devil enters God's project and suggests to Jesus how he could concretely carry out the role of *subject.* Thus, the devil would be another figure of the *sender*, a duplicate of the Spirit of God, whose narrative function would merely be that of reminding the subject of his contract. We could indeed be deceived into believing that it is so; certainly this impersonation is part of the "personage" of the devil. But are we certain to have accounted for all the operations of the text? More specifically, is it enough, in order to record the value of "If you are the Son of God . . . ," to translate it into three successive and ordered tests? Of course not. We must take into account the "suspension" realized by placing the divine sonship in a *conditional form*.

The devil's suggestion is more than the proposal of a dubious way for Jesus to reveal his origin. In fact, the devil's discourse aims at either denying or destroying Jesus' divine sonship. This actual purpose of the devil is clear in the third temptation, ". . . if you fall at my feet and worship me." The "if," the first word of the devil's discourse, represents an inversion of all that he seems to borrow from God's discourse. This transformation puts a negative sign on the whole proposed narrative program. We can summarize the preceding discussion as follows:

"IF"	Contract	Qualifying			
	Father	*Test*			
	Son	NS1			
		NS2			
		NS3			
		"Word"	*Main*		
			Test		
			NS1		
			NS2		
			NS3		
			"Bread"	*Glorifying*	
				Test	
				NS1	
				NS2	
				NS3	
					"Acknowledgement"

"If" would be, therefore, an operator of active negation. It is, in effect, a demonstration of the contrary; the series of tests would lead to the denying of what should have been affirmed. The devil does not deny openly the divine sonship of Jesus. Rather, he skillfully proposes to Jesus that he himself demonstrates that this sonship does not exist by accepting the devil as his sender. Such is the *anti-contract* suggested by the *anti-sender*.

At the level of the narrative as a whole, the entire sentence can be recorded as a single function: a *negative mandating*. The story of the temptation in the Gospel has its meaning as an "overture" which precedes and prefigures the actual tests and as a meta-linguistic summary of the temptations which will confront the hero. We witness here a significant disruption of the narrative statement by the enunciation. It appears that the program implied in the sentence, "If you are the Son of God . . . " is decisive even though it might seem to be harmless and even appealing.

It is possible that the formal aspect of the Greek text emphasizes the inconsequential and misleading character of this verse: εἰ υἱὸς εἶ τοῦ θεοῦ. Being and its negation are almost identical. Jesus' existence will unfold under the sign of this veiled contradiction and of the difficult choice that he will now openly express.

Lexie 5   But he replied: Scripture says . . .

The function "mandating" corresponds to that of acceptance or refusal. Here, the refusal of the negative mandating signifies the acceptance and remembrance by the hero of the positive mandating. This is how we must understand the verb "replying" and the allusion to the Scripture (γέγραπται) which reflects the contract binding Jesus to his Father. As a consequence of this refusal, the negative contract is not established and the proposed tests are nullified. The devil's program of action against the divine sonship of Jesus is neutralized. Yet, a detailed study of Jesus' answer shows that it is more than a mere return to the point of departure.

Lexie 6
Man does not live on bread alone but on every word that comes from the mouth of God.

Jesus borrows his response from Scripture (Deut 8:3). Consequently, his affirmation does not simply belong to the immediate and present enunciation but also to a past, "other," written enunciation. As we shall see below, this transformation gives to the reply a directness and a power particularly well adapted to the situation and to the opponent.

The sentence includes three processes:

— "Man does not live on bread alone." A relation of need or desire is established between man as subject and the bread as object. This relation is transformed by a partial negation (transformation of status).

— Man lives on something else: the Word. It is the same relation in a positive status.

— The Word comes from the mouth of God. This is a process which is converted into a qualification indicating origin.

The functional and actantial analysis reveals the following statements:

1) A statement of attribution (NS3) Function — communication, sender — X, object — life, receiver — man.

This statement is transformed by the operation of relativization which shows this attribution to be insufficient. The evoked test is therefore partly deceitful. The sender is denoted "X" because of the metaphoric and metonymic character of the reality through which the sender is manifested: the bread. We could say that the sender is the set, nature + culture. Both the values and goods which man receives from nature and those which result from human activities are insufficient: man cannot live by them alone. It should be noted that "bread" ($\check{\alpha}\rho\tau o\varsigma$) and the above "loaves" ($\check{\alpha}\rho\tau o\iota$) do not have the same actantial role; the singular is general, the plural is specific. One could reconstruct the complete performance as NS1 and NS2, that is, a continuous, more or less deceptive struggle by which man does or does not attain Life.

2) A statement of attribution (NS3) Function — communication, sender — God (his Word), object — life, receiver — man.

It is the same statement reestablished in its entirely positive status with a new actant: God manifested in his Word.

What happens in this part of the text? We can note first that there is a different investment of the actantial model. Instead of Jesus as receiver, we now find *man* — man understood in its most universal sense, as defined by the human condition. For the first time, Jesus refuses to remove himself from the human condition. Instead of Jesus as sender substituting his own order for the natural order, we now have the only authentic sender, God from whom man can receive the plenitude of life.

In the sentence there is also a disjunction (more semantic than syntactic) of the *bread* and the *Word*. They represent two orders for the communication of life. A hierarchy is established between these two orders. The bread represents the order of a deceitful test by lack of qualification — it is the order of what is insufficient; the *Word* represents the order of fulfilling the lack — it is the order of the necessary supplement. This network of orders is further complicated by the superimposition of another set of relations. The order of "stones, word, bread" in verse 3 is transformed when Jesus imposes the inverse order, "bread, word." No longer is it "his" word nor an "appropriate" word which would substitute bread for stones; rather, it is a word restored to its divine origin, which unmasks the insufficiency of bread. This transformation is not merely a return to word; it shows the way beyond bread.

We can ask, what does Jesus say about his divine sonship that the devil puts in question? Nothing directly. Apparently he transforms the question by putting "man" first and redefining himself in terms of the sole human condition. Yet, this answer specifies the very terms in which the question of his divine sonship can be raised: not in terms of bread but in terms of the Word which "comes from the mouth of God." There shall be in his existence an "order of the Word" to which his divine identity mysteriously belongs. It is by accepting entry into this order as a man — rather than using this word for his own sake — that he leaves open the matter which the devil wanted to close by means of an immediate and destructive affirmation. To the tempter's proposition, "If you are the Son of God . . . " Jesus responds by dismissing the immediate nomination (the title) in order to manifest the "locus" in which the reality of his identity can and will be revealed. This operation which will affirm Jesus' divine sonship is manifested figuratively as "inscription," as Scripture.

What we find in this verse is, perhaps, nothing other than a reminder of the affirmation found in the story of the Baptism in which Jesus is presented as the "Beloved Son." Yet, this direct proclamation is made by a "voice from heaven." It is not possible to recognize the sonship of Jesus as an obvious fact which belongs to this world and thus the affirmation is transformed by the way in which it is enunciated. The sonship of Jesus is removed from the human space, from human sight, and is now shown to belong to the order of the faceless "Voice," a missing signified (*signifié absent*) which, nevertheless, is necessary and is registered in the signifier (*significant*) as a lack, as an empty slot. "Who is He. . . ?" Only by means of a series of signifiers is it possible to reach the "locus" of the Son of God. The other alternative, to know fully who is "the Beloved Son," would be to identify the point of origin of the enunciation as the Father.

Lexie 7

The devil then took him to the holy city and made him stand on the parapet of the Temple . . . he said (to him) . . .

We find here a process of movement, a change of scene, and a communication involving the same actors. There are two canonic statements:

1. A statement of *movement*. Subject — Jesus, function — movement.

2. A *contractual* statement. Function — mandating, sender — the devil, receiver — Jesus, object — NS1.

The devil causes Jesus to perform the movement. These two statements are integrated in a manner similar to the statements in verse 1, "Jesus was led . . . out into the wilderness . . ." Thus the devil keeps his position as anti-sender as he is still attempting to assign inverse roles. There is a question here about Jesus' acceptance of this mandate. Does the fact that he moves imply that he accepts the contract proposed by the devil? No. The counter-proposition is not yet formulated. What Jesus accepts by following the devil to Jerusalem and later to the mountain is nothing other than what he has previously accepted by going into the wilderness "led by the Spirit." The presence of the anti-sender with him is part of the human condition in a world in which everything is ambiguous (*double jeu*), in which everything is performed following an ever-renewed choice, in which man is what he chooses to be. Under other circumstances Jesus will go to Jerusalem and to the Temple without following a suggestion of Satan. The effect of cancellation of the journey to the wilderness by this return to the city shows that the place where Jesus is found is always the place of confrontation between the two senders. See our interpretation of verse 1. The fulfillment of the positive contract and the glorification of the hero will coincide with a decisive movement which will challenge the value of the Gospel "loci." In the meantime, all the movements of Jesus take place within the ambiguous space of the risk. On this topic see the first part, "Les lieux du récit" of Louis Marin's book, *Sémiotique de la Passion.*

Lexie 8

If you are the Son of God . . . throw yourself down; for Scripture says: He will put you in his angels' charge, and they will support you on their hands in case you hurt your foot against a stone.

The devil's proposal begins with the same formula as in verse 3. The general structure is stable. In the first part, the series of processes is identical: "If you are the Son of God, throw yourself down . . . " The proposed action is different. It is no longer a matter of turning stones into loaves, but of throwing oneself down from the top of the Temple in a spectacular "parachute jump" to succeed because of the intervention of Angels mobilized in the service of the Messiah. We could repeat here all that we said about verse 3. The statements are similar in form and organization. It is a condensed story of what is proposed to Jesus, a mirror image of three tests which, according to the devil, would demonstrate Jesus' divine sonship.

We have to note also how the test makes use of the quotation from Psalm 91:11-12. It is as if the devil, measuring the impact of the Scripture upon Jesus, intended to use this "trump card" in his own game. His first proposition was intended to capitalize on Jesus' hunger. The second, by using these verses, hopes to capitalize on Jesus' respect for the authority of Scripture. The aim of the potential main test, expressed above in terms of stones being turned into loaves, becomes here the triumphal outcome anticipated by Scripture of the movement: "Throw yourself down . . ." This statement of attribution is modalized in the future tense so as to coincide with the narrative proposition of a contract and is further transformed by the operation of enunciating, "Scripture says." Consequently, the devil's proposition and God's contract (already accepted by Jesus) are identified with each other at the surface level. However, it is an apparent and not an actual identification. Indeed, when Satan presents in his discourse the outcome of the main test — and thus the power which shall insure the subject's domination — he hides himself behind the "enunciating position" as Jesus had in his first answer. The interlocking of the two contracts confuses the situation. For indeed the devil is absent from his own discourse in which Scripture, in an inverted position, is introduced. Thus, the devil's counter-proposition seems authentic and right. Scripture plays the same role as Jesus' hunger did in the first temptation — that of *helper*.

Lexie 9
Jesus said to him, Scripture also says: . . .

As in Lexie 5, due to the refusal of the mandating the contract is not established and the tests proposed by the devil are cancelled. But the form of the temptation demands an appropriate answer. Now, a mere appeal to Scripture is not sufficient. Indeed, Jesus intends to be absent from his own discourse by identifying his own enunciation which is somehow exterior to him. Yet, in so doing, he must avoid moving into the locus defined by the devil in the preceding verse. He must reestablish the truth about the locus from which Scripture transmits the Father's mandating. This change of locus is manifested by the adverb, "also," which expressed the multiplicity of the loci in Scripture. Metonymy for metonymy, Deut 6:16 represents Scripture as well as Psalm 91:11-12 . . . Furthermore, "Scripture says also" suggests that the various loci of Scripture are not necessarily equivalent, at least in terms of their literary meaning. One locus can cancel, relativize, or correct another. Thus, appealing to Scripture does not fully cover up the first locus of enunciation. The Scripture quoted by the devil does not become Word of God . . . It is Word of God for Jesus because of the locus in which he sets himself when reading it.

Lexie 10

You must not put the Lord your God to the test.

"Putting to the test" which links "you" with "God" in a negative form as an interdiction ("must not") is a single process. "Putting to the test" implies the function of mandating as we have noted *à propos* verse 1. The actant *sender* is represented by "you," i.e., the one to whom the word is addressed. In Deuteronomy, "you" is Israel. Here, it might be either the devil as interlocutor of Jesus or Jesus himself if he is viewed as responding from the vantage point which the devil assigned to him and from which he listens to the word of God. The *receiver* is the Lord. The statement could be written as follows: X (you) proposes a contract to God. This is almost to say that X has God at his disposal. It is not surprising that in Scripture such a statement has a negative form. It is unthinkable that somebody be the sender of God, i.e., that somebody dictates to God a program of action and imposes upon him a dependent volition. This is a contradiction in terms since before God man can only be *receiver* as Jesus already pointed out in his first answer. Man's attempt to establish himself as sender becomes a futile effort — either to use for his own sake the object transmitted by God or to deny the actual sender — by becoming his own sender (a "self-sender"). Despite all appearances, the devil's proposition implies an indirect negation of God himself. It is indeed the anti-God who confronts Jesus. In suggesting to Jesus that he should himself create the conditions under which he would be the beneficiary of the guarantees promised to the Messiah in Psalm 91, the devil actually proposes to Jesus that he become the anti-receiver of an anti-sender. This is further shown by the fact that Psalm 91 does not demand the messianic interpretation given to it by the devil. The divine protection is promised to any righteous man.

By introducing in this situation a saying of Deuteronomy, which earlier belonged to another controversy, Jesus does more than merely refuse the anti-contract of the devil. He suggests that insofar as the word and its negative performancial value (that is, the interdiction of testing God) are concerned he, Jesus, is in the position of sender. He can say to the devil: "You must not put to the test . . . " But, at the same time, he sets himself a second time in the human condition: It is because he is the receiver which accepts the word and the command of God that he can be sender *vis-à-vis* the devil. Thus, Jesus defines himself as a man among other man who can identify himself with the "you" of the Deuteronomic saying by entering into the order of the law (i.e., of the interdiction). He will not throw himself from the parapet of the Temple. But he does not refuse because he is afraid to submit to the law of nature which forecasts a tragic end for such an action; he will accept falling and being broken into pieces (cf. Matt 24:2, Luke 20:18). Rather, he refuses because of his decision to carry out the burden of the twofold law — the law of nature and the law of God — which is for men the only locus of the revelation of the Father. The preceding comments already belong to a semantic analysis which should be pursued by a discussion of the value of the possessive pronoun "your" (God) which expresses what has been traditionally called a "theology of the covenant." We shall leave this question open so as to respect the useful distinction between syntactic and semantic analysis.

Lexie 11

Next, taking him to a very high mountain, the devil showed him all the kingdoms of the world and their splendour . . . he said (to him) . . .

We find three processes. The first two can be analyzed as in Lexie 7:

— A movement proposed, accepted, and performed.

— A mandating and a proposition of contract.

— The third one is slightly different from the corresponding process in Lexie 7. "The devil showed to Jesus all the kingdoms of the world . . ." would correspond to "made him stand on the parapet of the Temple." In our analysis of Lexie 7, we implied that these details manifested in specific terms the function of movement and are not to be viewed as a distinct function. Here, by contrast, the verb "showing" includes a function which cannot be reduced to a movement, even though it expresses conjunction with an object. It is the attribution of an object according to the modality of sight (*regard*). Of course, seeing is to possessing what a proposition is to its actualization. Once more, we are at the stage of the mandating. The first temptation took shape on the basis of the hunger of Jesus — a lack being viewed as the locus of a potential fulfillment. The second temptation took place on the basis of the representation of the fall which called forth the image of a miraculous protection. Similarly, the third temptation takes shape on the basis of seeing the spendor of the earthly kindoms in contrast to Jesus' loneliness and poverty.

Lexie 12

I will give you all these, if you fall at my feet and worship me.

This third proposition is similar to and different from the preceding propositions. We find the same anticipation of the tests and their consequences in a micro-narrative modalized in terms of potentiality and proposition: "Jesus worships the devil who gives him power." The clearest function is that of attribution: the devil (sender) transmits (function) the power (object) to Jesus (receiver). Which test is it — a glorifying, main, or qualifying test? It is difficult to decide. The process of worshiping seems to represent the acceptance of the contract proposed by Satan and the forsaking of the prior contract linking Jesus to God . . . Worshiping would indicate that Jesus is displaced from the role of subject to the role of anti-subject. We could interpret this narrative stage — the entrance of Jesus in the negative side of the actantial model — as the main test. Yet, there are several problems with this interpretation. First, the qualifying test (establishment of the contract) would have been completely assimilated into the main test (confrontation). In other words, the domination of the negative subject would have taken place without any helper. Second, the attribution of power would not exactly correspond to the attribution of the *object-value*, but would rather be a prolongation in the order of the glorification. Thus, it seems better to recognize that the structure of this third proposition is not exactly parallel with that of the first two propositions. Furthermore, its form is different. The formula, "If you are the Son of God," is absent; a gift from the devil himself is mentioned; the action proposed to Jesus is oriented directly toward the devil. "Worshiping the devil" represents the acceptance of the mandating and the establishment of a negative contract; Jesus becomes anti-subject. The qualifying test with the gift of earthly power as helper follows. There is nothing more except that the object-vigor (of the qualifying test) is also object-value (of the main test) and object-message (of the glorifying test). The three objects are given in one as a metaphor of the infernal circularity, of the absolute dead end, and of the tautological character of the diabolic formulation itself. All is in all, nothing progresses, everything is closed upon itself because of the proposed action. "Worshiping the devil" contains the negation of the divine sonship. Radically separating Jesus from his origin and from his sender, this action forecloses against any possibility of manifesting the Father. Everything falls back into the opaqueness of the "glory of the kingdoms of this world." Thus, the mention of the divine sonship as helper or as object-message is useless as would be any allusion to God's action.

In fact, this third temptation is the manifestation of the true meaning and purport of the two preceding ones. The devil's suggestions that Jesus should change stones into loaves and that he should throw himself down from the Temple were, in fact, requesting Jesus to worship him. According to the devil, this relationship would bear the following fruit: a power totally homogeneous with the earthly sphere, a domination over nature and human societies without any other horizon. It would not be possible any longer for life and history to manifest the lack in which the presence-absence of God could be read. The main and spontaneous goal of the tempter is to satisfy, to eradicate, to fulfill, to kill the infinite desire: "All these I will give you . . . " Then Satan could retire in peace, confident that he has nothing any longer to fear from this void, this "wilderness," this desire, this hunger which he abhors since in it God manifests himself in the human reality.

Lexie 13

Then Jesus replied "Be off, Satan! For Scripture says: . . . "

The refusal of the mandating is more explicit and more brutal than before. It represents the meaning and the radicalness of the preceding refusals. As was suggested in the second response, Jesus has at his disposal a word which enables him to send Satan away — the word of the sender who assigns the roles as God can do. The Scripture in which the initial contract is found is also, in his mouth, a word of power, a quasi-helper which insures his victory over the tempter, which performs the disjunction from the anti-sender and thus reestablishes in the right way what was inverted by the "satanic mirror."

Lexie 14

You must worship the Lord your God, and serve him alone.

This is the vigorous affirmation of a contract which links "you" to God and defines the program of the subject. This contract is the exact opposite of Satan's project; God and God alone is recognized as sender and mandator.

It should be noted that the quotation from Scripture does not challenge the promise of Satan nor its object (the consequence of the test) as the first and second responses do, although the second answer does it less clearly than the first one. The proposed act is refused in and of itself and not because of its result or its goal. This suggests once again the relation of metaphor and metonymy which link this third temptation to the two preceding ones.

Our remarks concerning the "you" in Lexie 10 apply here as well. Jesus is himself when he welcomes and accepts the divine mandate, as the people of Israel and any man are constituted by the receiving and accepting of the divine mandate. He refuses to withdraw from the human condition by expressing his own status by reference to the people of the past, and he already suggests the status of the community which he shall become. Thus, the third answer makes explicit what was partially expressed in the preceding answers and reveals their total import.

Lexie 15
Then the devil left him.

This is a function of disjunction which is the inverse of that found in verse 3: " . . . and the Tempter came . . . " It is a signal at the narrative level that the series of functions is closed. The anti-sender is no longer on stage for the purpose of establishing the one which God has introduced as his "Beloved Son" in the post of anti-subject.

Lexie 16
And angels appeared and looked after him.

This is a function of conjunction which connotes movement. The actantial role of the angels remains vague. Because of the symmetry, we can nevertheless suggest that the angels are a figure of the positive sender. This is confirmed by the function of attribution implied in the mention of the "service" of the angels. The lack which affects Jesus will always be the locus of the manifestation of the One who sends him. The fact that the "service" of the angels is not described further suggests the communication of an undefined object which can never be identified as bread, triumph, or earthly glory.

Note on the Temptation Story in Luke

In the text of Luke, the three temptations are in a different order: the turning of the stones into loaves — the domination of the kingdoms of the world — the fall from the top of the Temple. The change of order has been well explained in terms of the author's intent, since for Luke, Jerusalem and the Temple have a distinctive symbolic value. Thus, Luke emphasizes the "journey to Jerusalem" (Luke 9:51-19:27) and concludes his Gospel narrative by a Temple scene (Luke 24:53). Similarly, he kept for the last and decisive victory of Jesus over Satan the temptation taking place at the Temple of Jerusalem. There is no need to come back to this point. But it would be useful to show the intrinsic balance of Luke's text and the specific relation of its various elements. In terms of an actantial and functional analysis, we would have to note that the inversion of the temptations provoked the suppression of the order, "Be off, Satan!" Since the tempter's departure is no longer correlated with this injunction, Luke introduces another statement: "Having exhausted all these ways of tempting him" (Luke 4:13). Thus, the third temptation of Matthew has lost, in Luke, its character of recapitulation. Because Satan himself initiates this departure, it becomes possible to mention his return: "The devil left him, to return at the appointed time" (Luke 4:13). Consequently, the relation of the temptation story to the whole Gospel and especially to the Passion story is manifested. The reader can expect to find in another time and place a repetition of what the devil has unsuccessfully attempted to realize here. It should also be noted that, according to Luke 4:6, the devil's domination over the world stands subordinated to a sender: All this power and glory of the kingdoms "has been committed to me and I give it to anyone I choose." The devil is indeed the anti-sender, but he is not the primary sender. Even though the relations remain undefined, the devil's role is assigned to him by somebody else. A last remark: the emphasis put upon the temptation at the Temple underscores the parallel Gospel scene (Luke 20:17-18), when Jesus, the "keystone" which will fall down, "will be dashed to pieces" and will take down with himself the Temple and the institution of which it is a metonymy.

CONCLUSIONS

We can now summarize the results of the twofold analysis that we have performed.

1. The Functional Scheme

The story of the temptation includes only functions which belong to the beginning of the syntagmatic model (i.e., the functions necessary for the establishment of the contract). The story exhausts itself in the attempt to establish the *anti-contract* and it does not go further than the *anti-mandating* which is each time refused. This text is almost an immobile narrative since it runs in a circle and returns to its starting point at the end. The potential tests remain imaginary and unreal. The micro-narratives, projected into the future by Satan, are cancelled by the obstinate reference to the deuteronomic narratives about the people of God. As a result, the positive contract which had been previously established and was again manifested at Jesus' Baptism is here reinforced.

2. The Actantial Scheme

The actantial scheme is characteristically twofold. The text manifests a few negative actantial positions around the anti-sender. Here, Jesus figures as the potential anti-subject but does not invest this position. The rest of the Gospel will show the change of Satan's aim. While he could not invest Jesus in a negative position, he will succeed in investing personages around

Jesus in his negative program. These personages will bring contradiction and confrontation in Jesus' ministry. The potential actantial investment is here manifested in its complexity so as to organize the various forces in conflict in the rest of the Gospel narrative. Thus, despite the apparent uselessness of this passage, we find in this text a micro-gospel inverted by the "satanic mirror" and "straightened up" by Jesus' word. At the heart of this confrontation is manifested the twofold question of *Jesus' identity* and of the *signification of Satan*.

Chapter II

Analysis of the Semantic Contents

a) Narrative Structures and Semantic Contents

The preceding analysis should not be construed as taking place outside the semantic field. First, its starting point is the meaning of the text as discovered through reading. Such an analysis deals with the "signified" of the text: consequently, it is already part of a semantic study. Let us not forget that the two methodological books of A. J. Greimas are entitled *Sémantique Structurale* and *Du Sens*! Second, what we have termed "narrative structures" and which can also be called "syntactic structures" (in view of their abstract and formal character which has some resemblance to "grammatical syntax") are not devoid of *meaning*. Where is the borderline between syntax and semantics? What is the nature of this distinction when, in the syntactic analysis of the narrativity we are constantly taking into consideration the compatibility and incompatibility among actantial roles and functions, and also studying the succession and logic of the syntagms and sequences? We have often alluded to the "content" — and at some length — so as to show more clearly the forms and their interplay. The distinction between these two types of analysis is therefore a matter of emphasis. One possible way to express the difference would be to say that the syntactic, or narrative, analysis corresponds to the analysis of the *syntagmatic* dimension of discourse. It is a quest for the models according to which a narrative unfolds, insuring in every instance the narrative's conformity to a network of relations which stands over each of its moments. This unfolding is the succession of figures (i.e., the variations permitted by the models) following one upon another. This is why we have preferred the title "narrative structures" for the first part of our analysis. The second part could then be said to belong to the analysis of the *paradigmatic* axis, a non-textual locus. This axis can be viewed as absent from the text, although it is either crossed by the text or crossing the text. It contributes to the construction of the meaning effect by leaving in the text the mark of its absence. *The paradigmatic axis is the theoretical locus of all the possible semantic units.* Thus, it includes the semantic units invested in the text and also all of those which could have been invested in the text. It is the "locus of intelligibility" of the discourse. The semantic analysis of the content refers to the paradigmatic dimension of the atoms, or the more or less complex molecules, of meaning. The analysis of the narrative structures can be viewed as referring to the functional and actantial models of the units of the syntagm. The two analyses are correlative; the narrative movement cannot be apprehended in a pure state, i.e., without a specific semantic investment. Similarly, the semantic content cannot be identified outside of the interplay of the narrative structures which manifest and establish the contrast and differences which call forth the paradigm as space favorable to the production of meaning.

Another way to express the difference between these two analyses could be proposed on the basis of the essay by A. J. Greimas and F. Rastier, "The Interaction of Semiotic Constraints" (*Yale French Studies*, 41, 1969, 86-105) and the essay by E. Benveniste, "Sémiologie de la langue" (*Semiotica*, 1969, 1-12 and 127-35). The analysis of narrative structures could be viewed as a *semiotic* study showing how the signs function, while the analysis of the content would be an actual *semantic* study dealing directly with the way in which the signified is structured in a discourse.

b) How to Proceed?

The preceding functional analysis provides us with the categories of the *contract* (established) and of the *anti-contract* (refused). The narrative does not unfold beyond this point. The micro-representations of the performancial sequences (tests) belong to Satan's propositions and are merely potential and anticipated narratives. Thus, the narrative structures perform only a few, very limited operations upon the contents. In order to explain these contents, we shall need to refer to the rest of the Gospel narrative.

The twofold actantial model provides us with a more complete network of relations which diffuses and reflects meaning and which regulates the image to image (or figure to figure) relations. Two actantial positions are emphasized, the anti-sender and the subject. The objects communicated remain more mysterious, yet it should be possible to identify them in their figuration as messages. It is around these privileged points that meaning appears. This observation suggests how to proceed.

We can focus our analysis upon the two main personages or actors and gather around them the loci and objects clearly manifested in the text as configurations of meaning. In fact, the order that we shall follow in our analysis does not matter so long as we keep in mind that it is impossible to explain a semantic content in and of itself. The semantic contents must be studied in their interrelation with each other; for *semes* are passed from one semantic unit to another as a result of the parallelism of the isotopies which can, to a certain extent, be reduced to each other.

c) The "Personage" in a Narrative

Since this analysis will be focused upon the *actors* (Jesus and Satan especially but also the Spirit, God, the angels, and man), it is important to dispel once more the impression that a personage is a "natural" rather than a literary construct. This illusion leads to the foreaking of the analytical attitude: *a priori* a personage is viewed as a narrative element which cannot be deconstructed. In such a case, the analysis in terms of the "codes" is suspended and the personages are studied only at the level of "speech" (in de Saussure's sense of the term) or of style. The fact that the literary personage is a construct was already shown by our analysis of the narrative structures. The personage is, at least in part, the product of the conversion of the functions which he performs or could perform into qualifications. Furthermore, the process of codification — inherent in any linguistic phenomenon

— involves a fixation of content at a specific level of complexity through the association of a signified with a specific signifier (a proper name or another designation). In this way, the signified is predetermined in various meaningful units and especially in words. This solidification of meaning is a phenomenon of *code* which greatly facilitates the function of communication of language because it eliminates the necessity for a permanent reconstruction of the meaningful units. By convention, a specific word is viewed as representing a specific state of *crystallization* and of combination of basic elements; it is a "molecule" which is recognized and has its place in a code. Yet this semantic molecule possesses a degree of indetermination. In fact, it is primarily the compatibilities and incompatibilities with other semantic units which are specified. This coded basis represents a useful and secondary "opening bid," an "outside" of the text which, by convenience, the reader apprehends as a "natural" given; its paradigm would be equivalent to a "dictionary." This army of signifieds previously constructed and identified as belonging to classes or codes (topographic code, onomastic code, hermeneutic code, etc. . . .) invades our text. Consequently, the story of the temptation appears as having been in great part pre-fabricated. The studies of this passage have often been focused on the "pre-text" rather than on the text itself. Without forgetting the role of the "code," we shall nevertheless attempt to free ourselves from this representation of the personage as known and knowable in itself prior to its figuration in the narrative.

Upon entering the discourse, the meaningful units are submitted to the interplay of the constraints discussed in the first part of this analysis. Under this pressure some atoms of meaning are separated from semantic molecules and are synchronically correlated with other atoms which belong to foreign semantic units. Other semantic features impose themselves, creating redundances and the phenomena of *isotopy*. Meaning is constituted on the basis of this complex interplay which involves the whole of the text. The intuition of the reader is thus correct — the message is the basic global unit, the interplay of structure is secondary. Yet, the continual passage back and forth from the global message to the articulation of the code is in fact nothing but the cover behind which much more complex operations take place. Behind this cover, the *full* units of the code are constantly reconverted into *relative* units according to the absolute law of the difference. The analysis must venture itself into this fluctuating universe in which the selection and the combination of the minimal semantic features is performed. In so doing, the analyst presupposes that the signified which is fixed at the level of the code and recorded in the lexicon is only one of the keyboards upon which is played the discursive process. In fact, these coded, fragmented, specified, and more or less fixed signifieds manifest their semantic value only if they are integrated at a wider semantic level. This semantic level, structured but not coded and thus more unstable, is coextensive with the discourse and produces the global meaning effect. It is at this level that the narrative organization and transformation of meaning are performed so as to define the semantic content specific to each text. Therefore, without denying the lexematic level (the level of the code, of the lexicon), the analysis must aim at identifying these discursive figures. For this purpose, the analyst must primarily investigate the phenomena of correlation, exchange, neutralization, inversion, etc. These phenomena create the semantic space, the horizon of meaning which cannot be identified with the sum of the specific meanings of the words. It can be expected that such an analysis will be quite different from the study of the personages in and of itself, i.e., from the establishment of a "portrait" which reinforces the illusion of subjectivity. These remarks about the personage apply as well to the analysis of the topography and of the objects in a narrative.

B. THE DEVIL — SATAN — THE TEMPTER

These three names refer to a single personage. His functional value is manifested in the third term. But this remark does not say much. It refers to the "semantic circle." What is it to tempt? There is no doubt that, according to the religious code of Israel, all these designations correspond to a signified crystallized in various Old Testament and apocryphal texts. Satan is not unknown when the story of the temptation begins. And, indeed, he will perform as expected! The determinations which he receives here, added to his pre-determinations, will become part of the figure of the devil in Christian literature. But all these remarks are not sufficient; they interpret the semantic units of the text exclusively in terms of the lexicon and not in terms of the *paradigm*. The analysis will aim at deconstructing this too well-known figure so as to grasp among its elements the atoms of meaning which can be identified (directly, after inversion or after various types of transposition) with atoms of meaning scattered in other parts of the text. Our analysis will be focused on the semantic features assumed in the narrative by the satanic pole and organized in an unstable but richer discursive configuration. Consequently, we shall not dwell heavily on the usual semantic values included in the lexemes "devil," "Satan," and "tempter." These configurations are stable but minimal. In order to apprehend the richness of the meaning effect of the satanic configuration, we need to consider it in terms of a much more general semantic field than the "satanic field." This is why we shall study the satanic personage in terms of the various fields manifested in this narrative.

The Anti-Sender

In this narrative, the devil is constantly an anti-sender. This actantial position is defined by its specific relations to the actantial model as a whole. It does not have any other semantic value than what differentiates it from the other actantial positions and especially from its inverse — the other sender. As long as we remain at the formal level, it is barely possible to speak of *anti-*sender or of *negative* sender. It is better to say that we are dealing with two *inverse* senders; the subsequent analysis of the semantic investment will determine which of the two is the "right" sender and which is the "inverse" sender. The personage of Satan includes this value of inversion vis-à-vis the Spirit and God. The text itself attributes this value to Satan. In the total semantic field, this value of the personage can be conceived as an *index of refraction*, i.e., a specific way of receiving, transforming, and sending back the semantic particles which are in movement in the narrative space. This index of refraction, although quite abstract, is a formative principle of the personage. It predisposes this specific personage to integrate better than any other the negative semes. Similarly, the "right" sender integrates better the positive semes. The first result of the introduction in a narrative of an inverse sender (negative sender) is that it provides a field of crystallization for the negative values which either complements a manifested field of positive values or at least determines the field of positive values. In this latter case, the narrative can delay or even forego a specific manifestation of the positive sender. This is what we find in our text: Satan's active presence in these first Gospel texts determines the "space" of the other sender which always needs to be "elsewhere" and absent-present:God. Satan is the inverse of God, the inverting and deforming mirror. But it should be clear that the formula cannot be turned around; God is not, in this text, the inverse of Satan. On the semantic axis of the *order*, God is first and Satan is second. Satan is always preceded in his speech by an anterior speech, by Scripture, by the voice at the Baptism which has established what he attempts to deny. Finally, in this confrontation, Satan is dismissed when Jesus, who was called to be subject, dominates the anti-sender by assuming himself the position of sender. Thus God is alone in the supreme position (4:10).

Thus, when the text speaks of Satan, is it somehow speaking of God? Apparently the Gospel of God in Jesus Christ does not have any other goal. But, in order to interpret this discourse about Satan correctly, we must define the laws of deformation of this diabolic image so as to cancel all the effects of inversion in his semantic field. In other words, when attempting the analysis of the personage Satan we must take into account the "index of refraction" of another actor in the position of subject — Jesus. Speaking of Satan is also speaking of Jesus, even though he does not invest the same actantial position as God. Thus, speaking of Satan is speaking of all the personages or, better, it is to let all the personages speak at once. The goal of our analysis is thus to give back to the text the possibility of speaking with its multifold voice — an impossible task, since the single voice which makes it possible invalidates it!

The Weight of the Signified

On the basis of these fundamental determinations, the narrative constructs the personage Satan and therefore also the others, into an image primarily by means of *discourses*: Satan speaks. He speaks to Jesus. Let us first deal with the value that the title, "Son of God," has in his mouth and with the way in which Satan establishes himself as locutor when using this title. We have noted above (in our interpretation of *lexie 4*) that the devil's proposition correlated and subordinated the unfolding of the main test (turning the stones into loaves — throwing himself down) to the explanation of Jesus' divine identity in the form of a possessed and recognized power. Thus, the formula, "If you are the Son of God," bestows to this knowledge and acknowledgment the value of first and necessary priority. Jesus is exhorted to seek exclusively this acknowledgment without delay in the present place and time (*hic et nunc*). He must make it known that he is the Son of God. He must establish himself in this privileged status and convince men that this is who he is. He must impose himself as the image of God in this world and, thus, establish God without ambiguity among the forces of nature and among human institutions. Using basic linguistic terminology, Louis Marin affirms correctly that this formulation manifests the tendency to dismiss the signifier in favor of the signified, which is considered as the only real value. Such an operation which seems favorable to the correct functioning of the linguistic sign and coherent with the mission of the Son hides, in fact, a fatal inversion. But, as we shall see below, Jesus will not be deceived and will give back to the signifier its priority.

The personage Satan is fundamentally determined by the

interplay of the opposition, "signifier vs. signified." Through the Gospel, he will remain a factor which dismisses the signifier and affirms the signified. When the figure of the devil is introduced in a narrative about Jesus, the focus changes and weight is immediately given to the signified, i.e., to the proclamation, in one form or another, of the divine sonship of Jesus. This is clear, for instance, in the casting out of the demons which Jesus has silenced (Mark 1:23-25), in the reactions of the Pharisees which involve an inversion (Matt 10:32-34), in Peter's answers (Matt 16:16 and 16:22-23), and in Judas' betrayal (although in this latter case, new elements are involved, permitting a true passage to the signified).

The third temptation shows this content of the personage "tempter." His propositions would bestow upon Jesus an exceptional position in the earthly order at the price of an acknowledgment of Satan as anti-God. Passing *hic et nunc* to the signified is equivalent to the affirmation of a false God. The anticipated affirmation of the signified implies indeed the negation of God; it is the breaking of the contract which aims at inscribing in human history the trace of the true God.

Presence vs. Absence

The same semantic value of Satan can perhaps be shown in terms of this other pair of oppositions. Indeed, what Satan intends to test is the presence or absence of God in Jesus. He wants to clarify the situation! "Tell us if you are the Christ, the Son of God . . . " (Matt 26:63), "Give us a sign . . . " When Jesus is present, is God present? Yes or no? Satan's attitude is strangely similar to our own attitude toward a signifier from which we demand the immediate revelation of its signified and which we are ready to send back into the darkness of meaninglessness if we do not obtain satisfaction. A signified, which by nature cannot be grasped, must be declared present or absent. Here, these concepts are not out of place, since we are dealing with a *sign* related to the revelation of the Son. Satan presupposes that God is the signified and that Jesus is the signifier. This disjunction is radically destructive of both God and man. First of all, why should the question of the divine identity of Jesus dismiss any true consideration of his human reality, i.e., of his actual life viewed from a human perspective? Furthermore, our relation to the signifier is not what is implied here. The subject is never a signified, even if it is God. The manifestation of the subject in the discourse is an endless alteration from presence to absence. The subject must become signifier among signifiers or it shall not be manifested.

The reader might want to object to this interpretation because the categories "absence vs. presence" and "signifier vs. signified" are not found in the text. This is true at the level of the manifestation. We introduce them at a metalinguistic level as a way of expressing how the personage of Satan and the meaning of several Gospel texts have been generated. Other semantic categories can be chosen. But it cannot be denied that the categories that we used so far fit the semantic network of the text. Could we go so far as to say that they are presupposed by the text?

Immanence vs. Transcendence

While pretending to anticipate the revelation of the sonship which defines Jesus' identity, Satan intends to pervert it. The semantic value of the devil is thus related to both the negative feature of his plan and to the feature, "now vs. later," which can be termed "here vs. elsewhere" or, even better, "immanence vs. transcendence." For Satan, it is already the time and place to pass from Jesus to the Son of God. What would be gained in the hurry? The Gospel will explain it: the Passion could be avoided. "This must not happen to you . . . " declares Peter before being rebuked, "Get behind me, Satan . . . " (Matt 16:22-23). In our text, this semantic interplay is indirectly manifested in the role of the tempter. First, Satan takes advantage of Jesus' lack of food. The devil presents to Jesus the object-lacked and the process which would insure its attribution. He proposes an immediate response to the need, an immediate cancellation of the lack. This characteristic feature of Satan could be registered on an axis, "full vs. empty," or "satisfaction vs. lack." In the space created by the absence of food the shadow of the bread-tempter (or of the "tempter-bread") appears. This shadow imposes the potential presence of bread and covers up any other reality which could enter into the field of desire because of this lack. The horizon shrinks. The desire must not remain without satisfaction, else it could invest with meaning another object which could be substituted for the material bread, thereby keeping only its metaphorical value. Satan cannot afford to take this risk for, indeed, such a metaphorical substitution could irresistibly manifest the deep identity of Jesus. Everything must disappear in order to become bread, and these stones first of all. For they are the "anti-bread" *par excellence* and thus could become the basis of a metaphor which would reveal the subject. If there must be a transformation, it is better that they be introduced in the field of the immediate need and become harmlessly a metonymy of bread.

Common Condition vs. Exception

The context of the second temptation is different: the holy city and the Temple. These are two places that Jesus will visit and he will be related to them both metonymically and metaphorically. From Satan's perspective, this subtle interplay must be controlled so that anything capable of revealing the deep identity of Jesus is brought under control. Any surprise must be avoided. Another form of desire is involved here, the desire of be recognized. When Jesus enters Jerusalem and the Temple, he enters his home. Everything has been prepared for his coming. Everything belongs to him. Everything speaks of him, proclaims his lordship, his filial right over his Father's domain. It is unthinkable that the encounter of the Son and of the "vineyard of God" in the presence of "vineyard workers" be not the locus of a decisive revelation of the filial identity. Thus, Satan must organize this encounter in his own way. The same categories structure the scenario — "immediately" without waiting for the "hour." The cunning is clear; the time is man! God is not subject to time. The first confrontation with Jerusalem and the Temple must be decisive and demonstrate once and for all who Jesus is. Immediate satisfaction of the desire is required and Jesus must not wait indefinitely for the acknowledgment of his people. His desire could change. The people must not remain in doubt. Once more, the signifier must immediately disappear so that the signified might appear: he is the Son of God! The signifier must be transparent. Any thickness of any figure of the signifier must be excluded so that the manifestation might be fully manifesting. Any materiality, any heaviness must be suppressed. Jesus must free himself without any delay from the common human laws which keep him in an insignificant silence, away from this point between heaven and earth where he will be able with one step to fall down into the realm of *meaning*. On the hands of angels he will then go over the barrier which separates his Nazarean name, "Jesus," from his heavenly title, "Son of the Father." Scripture has anticipated this royal plunge, this instantaneous change of scene which will expose God to the sight of the amazed spectators who, for centuries, had been called to witness the last scene of the show. This will be the satisfaction and the success. Any failure and any opposition is excluded. The rest will necessarily follow.

Satisfaction vs. Lack — Need vs. Desire

During its third stage, the temptation takes a global character and deals with a third dimension of desire. There is a new element in this last proposition of the tempter which is the manifest conjunction of Satan with the power and the glory of the kingdoms of this world. Luke specifies: "for it has been committed to me" (Luke 4:6). When Satan proposes to Jesus the global object — "all these" — which, accordingly should satisfy the main need of his interlocutor, he in fact aims at suppressing any desire in him, at cancelling any difference which could signify Jesus' transcendent identity. Now, after the unsuccessful attempt at misleading Jesus concerning the means through which God's presence can be manifested to men, Satan aims at limiting Jesus to a primary role of earthly domination. He proposes to Jesus that he be a super-signifier. This is indeed the best and most convincing way to reduce God to man; God would be an absurd signified disguised in a super-signifier.   Then, there would not be any gap left and, thus, no room for word and speech. In the space delimited by this proposition which is apparently favorable to God, the truth appears. It is the choice of another God, of the anti-God, which is proposed to Jesus: " . . . If you fall at my feet and worship me . . . " Such is the only God able and willing to set himself up in the first place of universal power. His revelatory signifier is borrowed from the splendor of the glory in which he is immersed and with which he can be confused. Yet, the face of this God (Satan!) is always elsewhere, always fleeting, always masked. He is the one who proposes the power and the glory and who offers himself as object of worship. He is the one who apparently wants to establish God in the world and who in so doing establishes himself in it despite all appearances.

When reduced to a more systematic formulation, this semantic value can be written as "satisfaction vs. lack," "immediacy vs. delay," "domination vs. submission," "exception vs. common condition," "need vs. desire," "splendid presence vs. meaningful absence," "seeming vs. being" . . .

The day will come when Jesus will be able to say, "All authority . . . has been given to me . . . " (Matt 28:18). But it will be a different hour. The Passion and the death will have established Jesus at the last place. He will have revealed God in submission and poverty and will have defeated the "Prince of this world." It is from the Father and from him only that Jesus will receive power. He will receive this, not in order to dominate, but in order to save, not in order to enjoy domination, but in order to open a new space for the Word ("Go, therefore, make disciples of all the nations . . ." Matt 28:19), not in order to take the place of men, but in order to be God with them, invisible and present.

Conclusions

When the function, "Departure of Satan," takes place, the manifestation of his semantic content is concluded in two ways. As anti-sender, he suspends his action vis-à-vis Jesus. For a time, says Luke: "to return at the appointed time" (Luke 4:13). In the narrative system, he keeps his value as a potential sender who

assigns the negative roles to other actors. He remains perpetually
the agent who inverts the helpers into opponents, who solicits
neutral attitudes, and initiates negative operations. After this
appearance in the front stage, everything suggests that he will now
work in the backstage according to the common rules which
govern the manifestation of any sender. Thus, Satan will ascribe
roles from the backstage and suggest to the actors on the front
stage the text of their discourse. The Gospel will register the
almost perfect echo of the tempter's proposals in the questions or
interpretations of the Pharisees, of the disciples, and even of
Peter, and at the last of Judas. Satan's departure opens the space
of "natural" ambiguity which characterizes the human condition
in which Jesus wants to live. Satan opens the time of the free
interplay of the requests transmitted by the realities which Jesus
will encounter daily. But, from now on, the situation is clear for
the reader of the Gospel because of the figuration of the anti-
sender in our text.

Finally, in Matthew's text, Satan does not depart on his own.
He obeys Jesus' order, "Be off, Satan!" This is more than a mere
stylistic formula. The roles are inverted. Jesus as sender organizes
the departure of Satan who will go away defeated and dominated.
He who appeared as the potential anti-subject identifies himself
with the sender and reintroduces into the text the category,
"subordination," of the anti-sender. Satan is not the symmetric
opposite of God (although he might be that of the angels who take
his place in the narrative). And Jesus has clearly revealed his own
identity without compromising at all with Satan. What can the
devil do when confronted with the Truth? Unwillingly, he
confirms it when he is dismissed. He is tricked by his own cunning,
and is suddenly deprived of his power which he preposterously
intended to transmit. He is left empty handed despite all that he
possesses.

The issue of the confrontation is different in Luke: "Having
exhausted all these ways of tempting him, the devil left him, to
return at the appointed time" (Luke 4:13). It is in himself that
Satan finds the reason for his departure. He has nothing else to

propose, he has exhausted his resources, and is, therefore, a ridiculous anti-sender. This situation of Satan emphasizes the stability of Jesus in the primary contract and implies that Jesus has indeed the power to carry it out to a meaningful conclusion according to his program.

C. JESUS

The problem raised by the semantic analysis of the personage Jesus is very complex. We first need to explain the semiological status of the proper name. Because he is constantly represented by his name ("Jesus" or various pronouns) and is never described or presented by any qualification (e.g., there are no adjectives applied to Jesus), it would seem that the main personage of the narrative cannot be analyzed. This is further reinforced by the fact that the referential value of the proper name, Jesus, is well known. At the beginning of chapter 4, everyone knows who Jesus is and what value should be given to each occurrence of his name. The reader does not raise any question about this aspect of the text. Everything is clear. Everything is "natural" and the decoding is smoothly performed. For the reader, since the term, "Jesus," designates without ambiguity a specific being, its semantic content is a given provided by an "onomastic code." There is apparently no need for a semantic de-construction. With the personage Satan this problem did not seem as acute because of the multiplicity of names and because one of them was functional (tempter). But, in fact, any word in the text presents the same difficulty which arises from the coded character of the language. For each signifier there is a corresponding signified with a small "free-play," a potential stylistic readjustment of the signified which is variously used by the speakers. Without this constraint of a well-defined and well-signaled network, we could not communicate with each other! Thus, what happens with the name Jesus happens also with all of the words of our discourses. The name Jesus simply refers to the code and to the situation in which the Gospel has been enunciated. The text has no analytical preoccupation. Furthermore, the proper name is semantically empty. Because it designates a single person it does not need to contain generic features and specific characteristics of a semantic class. By definition, it is not a common name, i.e., a name common to several elements of a class. Its value does not designate any other concept. It is not defined and does not define what it represents. It designates and does not do anything else. This character of the proper name explains why it is almost impossible to make a discourse out of it. In some cases, it is possible to speak of its etymology and of its symbolic value. This is done with Jesus' name, "God saves." This etymological meaning does not help much in the understanding of this text. But, the commentator in most instances leaves the name aside and speaks of the person who is designated in a psychological discourse built upon the basis of textual features. Yet, the Gospel does not provide sufficient psychological features for developing such a discourse. We shall try to avoid both the etymological and the psychological types of interpretation so as to present a strictly semiotic analysis. Whoever may be the person designated by this name, a literary personage is generated in the Gospel narrative by the interplay of semantic units. Its coded value represents a minimal figure common to a series of texts. We must show what the discursive figure produced by this passage is and what the laws of its construction are. For this purpose, we can use all of the functions manifested in the text since they can be converted into qualifications.

We can add to the difficulties mentioned above those produced by the actantial status of Jesus. Jesus' actantial position is not symmetrical to Satan's. Jesus is invested by the Spirit of God in the position of subject for a complex mission which will include the manifestation of his real identity (cf. the Baptism). Satan proposes to him a potential anti-contract. Thus, Jesus alone is in the position of subject. It is possible to discover in him all of the relations which can eventually represent the values ascribed to Satan. We need to go back to a detailed analysis.

As he first appears on the stage, Jesus manifests the positive sign, i.e., the sign of God whose mandate he has accepted. But he does not possess this sign as the sender does (or as the anti-sender possesses the negative sign). His role as subject establishes him in a position of *received* positivity and of proposed negativity. Furthermore, he is not alone in the adventure. He is responsible for the transmission of the object-value to the receivers. With him the object and the receivers enter the horizon of the text. And, because the narrative chooses to attempt the perversion of the subject into an anti-subject rather than investing another actor with this position, it is the same actor who will manifest and deny the anti-subject and the anti-receivers. Such complexity makes the analysis difficult.

We have established a pertinent semantic axis, the existential status. It includes two categories: "determined (fixed) vs. chosen" (these categories might be reduced to "static vs. dynamic," "given vs. acquired" . . .). In the text, Jesus is the figure of the category *choice* — he chooses to be such and such. He chooses who he will be (including Son of God) and the mode of this existence. This total freedom is the direct opposite of the satanic perspective: "If you are the Son of God . . ." Jesus deliberately establishes himself in the process of signification and not in the immobility of the signified. This is an anticipated conclusion that we need to establish by a systematic analysis.

The Forty Days

A *first* observation can be made about the fast of forty days and forty nights. The conclusion of our preceding analysis (cf. above *Lexie 2*) was that this process includes three functions organized in the syntagm of a text refused by the subject. We found it difficult to identify the opponent to be confronted and the sender of the food, although we suggested "nature and society." Through this process Jesus separates himself from the natural and cultural order which permits the physical survival of man. The meaning effect is threefold. It includes first the feature, "exceptional vs. normal." Jesus sets himself in an exceptional situation. This feature is to be contrasted with the explicit will of conformity to the common condition expressed elsewhere in the text. But this exception does not aim at the same thing. Indeed, there is a second feature which can be noted: "fragile vs. solid," "precarious vs. guaranteed." Jesus takes a risk when he deprives himself of food. His separation from the ordinary sender of life implies the expectation of another sender who is not apparent and not yet recognized. Jesus has no intention of forcing the intervention of this other sender. Quite to the contrary, he is ready to accept the consequences and the weight of deprivation. Finally, a third feature: the absence of the object-food where the need is opens a problematic space which represents a void, a deprivation, and the sign of a horizon within which the unsatisfied need is inverted, becoming another figure that we can call (by convention) "desire." Jesus wants something other than food, or to put it in terms of food, Jesus wants a food other than bread, another kind of bread. He is expressing here a need which is different from the needs that nature or society can satisfy. In Jesus, man is confronted with his true reality. All this is fairly well represented in the spatial code by the location, "wilderness." To this is added the temporal notation, "delay" — "He fasted for forty days and forty nights." This duration has a symbolic value which can be understood as a quotation. Apart from its coded value, we must consider this notation of time in itself. Jesus takes for himself a length of time and thus gives a signification to time. Thus, the text can make use of the opposition, "now vs. delay," which is parallel to that represented in the wilderness, "here vs. elsewhere." Because "delay" is in conjunction with "need," we can even say that the opposition should read "now vs. late." Therefore, it appears that the reference to "time" in Jesus' horizon might be a first figuration of death. Furthermore, the conjunction of "time" with "desire" also produces the figure of the delayed by truthful revelation of the identity. Such is the subject that Satan attempts to introduce in his own relational network by proposing an anti-contract to him.

The Bread or the Word

We know how the first temptation deals with the situation of *lack*, i.e., by suppressing the desire through an immediate satisfaction, even though it pretends to be a clear demonstration of the divine power of Jesus. The refusal of this mandate reestablishes the normal order of the relations according to the positive actantial scheme. The form in which this refusal is presented is most interesting for the semantic analysis.

Jesus is absent as much as possible from his own discourse, which is reduced to a quotation from Deuteronomy introduced by the stereotyped formula, "Scripture says." Let us emphasize that we are not discussing Jesus' intentions nor the Gospel writers' intentions, but exclusively the semantic network of the text. There are no explicit signs of the enunciation here, e.g., the first or second person personal pronoun. We would not have been suprised by a response like, "I am not here in order to . . . " in which the "I" would have been the formal mark of the subject of the enunciation. But we do not find anything like this. The manifestation of Jesus' subjectivity is reduced to a minimum. It is not around him that his representation of the real is built. Thus, we find here the opposition, "marked enunciation vs. non-marked enunciation." If in the text we find other manifestations of this opposition in the text, we may be led to substitute for its linguistic categories the more explicitly semantic categories: "explicitly signified identity vs. guarded identity (or identity hidden in the signifier)."

The choice of the quotation seems to confirm the preceding suggestion. Jesus avoids quoting a messianic text. Between the sender, "God," the object, "Word," and the receiver, "man," there is no place for the subject, "Jesus." On the contrary, he seems to assimilate himself to the position of man who, beyond a quest for bread, desires and receives the Word. This principle which applies to any man also applies to Jesus. What is written in Scripture, more precisely in the *Law* (Deuteronomic torah), is the order to which Jesus refers to himself as his people do. It is in this context

that Jesus can truthfully define himself, rather than in the context
of the exclusive relationship between the Son and the Father. The
desire for the Word is manifested in the physiological demand for
bread ("he was very hungry"). As if the text were coming back
upon itself, this desire for the Word is presently satisfied, not in a
privileged, face to face relationship with the Father, but rather in
the universal signifance of Scripture which is above this
relationship, precedes it, and surrounds every man. Or, better, it is
in Scripture that Jesus finds and recognizes himself as a man
among men, and it is in this total context that he discovers himself
as Son of the Father of all. Here we would need to analyze the text
of the Baptism so as to emphasize the role of the presence of the
Spirit who reappears at the beginning of the Temptation story.
We would also need to note that the Spirit is like a dove; this
feature specifies the conditions in which the revelation of the
beloved Son takes place (Matt 3:16-17).

Thus, in this brief discourse of Jesus the conditions and the
modalities of the manifestation of the subject are drawn. It is an
immense metaphor attempting to express what cannot be uttered,
suggesting that "what cannot be uttered" belongs to a "beyond,"
manifesting its absence and its mark, and hiding it when
manifesting it. It is by clothing himself in the garb of the most
anonymous discourse of Scripture and in the garb of the most
common human condition that Jesus intends to affirm himself as
the only Son of the Father. Priority is given to the signifier, while
the attitude vis-à-vis the signified is guarded.

This movement from Jesus to man is correlated in the text with
the more explicit conjunction of the Word with the bread. We
have seen that when it is manifested in this way, the truth about
man also expresses the truth about Jesus. It is the Word of God
that Jesus desires, and he does not care for Satan's proposition.
Thus, he refuses the miraculous bread. But the text does not stop
here. The text implicitly refers back to Jesus' actantial position as
subject with the mandate to transmit to men the object of their
desire. In this way, the text designates the Word of God as the
object-value which defines Jesus' mission. Sent by God, he must

first of all transmit the Word and not bread. Of course, the one does not exclude the other: "Man does not live on bread *alone*. . ." It is the disjunction which is an impossibility and which denies man. Maybe we should add, no Word without bread. Indeed, Jesus will not ignore the need for bread that others experience (cf. the feeding of the five thousand). But this is not his deep identity. He must put in conjunction with the bread the desired Word. He intends to give to any man the possibility that he himself experienced in the wilderness where he was fed by Scripture. Accepting Satan's proposal would be separating the Word from the bread and thus offering to men a bread transformed into stone. Refusing this proposal, he will be Word accompanying the bread. He will not give bread for, in so doing, he would risk reducing to a physiological need a desire related to the communion of persons. It is in this way that he will be man and that he will be Son of God. He has chosen.

It is difficult to express in semantic categories what is manifested in these figures of meaning: "conjunction vs. disjunction" or "desire vs. need" as applied to the Word and the bread; "nature and culture vs. a third dimension related to the communion of persons . . . " It is clear that the formation of the semantic level of the discourse takes place above the lexemes and beyond the constraints of the code. It would be fruitless to analyze independently the two lexemes "word" and "bread!" But when these are analyzed together an opposition appears: "the bread goes *in* the mouth of man vs. the word which goes *out* of the mouth of God." These categories are especially meaningful when they are considered together with the opposition, "nature and culture vs. intersubjective communication."

By refusing the program of the transformation of stones into loaves, Jesus implicitly defines his filial identity. He suggests that the manifestation of his relation to the Father is not the transmission of a truth different from himself or different from the object-value that he must communicate to men. Satan had singled out the "sonship formula" in order to ask for its demonstration. Jesus denies the possibility of demonstrating his filial identity in this way: first, he suppresses from his own discourse the formula itself and any reference to an exceptional status and, second, he reintroduces the question of his identity in the evocation of his mission and of his condition. The Word, which he is associating with the bread of men, "comes from the mouth of God." From this we cannot deduce anything about Jesus' divine identity. But the figure of his true identity is positively drawn. Jesus shall speak. His word will accompany the bread. One day, his word will become bread. And, mysteriously, as a subject is present in a series of words, as the real identity of somebody can be suggested by his discourse, he who speaks will be recognizable and recognized . . . but he will also suddenly disappear. Thus, the movement — from the word to the bread which links men to God through his Son — cannot cease. This is the whole Gospel (cf. especially Luke 24:13-35) which will unfold what the story of the Temptation expresses discreetly.

The stones of the wilderness must remain stones. Upon them the words of Scripture utter the truth of human desire and the insufficiency of earthly food; no other sign will be given to men. It will be the sign of Jonah because such a choice of lateral, metaphoric manifestation which is nothing other than a patient and simple work for the service of men, leads to the cancellation and the exchange of signifiers (see the second part of Louis Marin's *Sémiotique de la Passion*). It is the same process which leads Jesus to manifest his own truth, to transmit his Spirit, and to disappear from the human horizon. As a mark of the unity of the Gospel text, when at the "appointed time" the signified will be manifested, the bread (eucharist), and the stone (of the Temple) will reappear.

The Temple and the Body

The second temptation first performs a kind of cancellation of the movement to the wilderness which modifies the signification of the "subject." For the first time in the Gospel according to Matthew (the situation is different in the Gospel according to Luke), Jesus in in conjunction with Jerusalem and Temple. He will be again in conjunction with them at the end of the synoptic narratives (Matt 21; Luke 19:28 ff.) and more frequently and earlier in the Gospel according to John. This conjunction will never be neutral, for in the Synoptics it primarily represents the main test. Satan or his representatives will be present.

The meaning effect has already been analyzed (cf. above *lexie 7*, and the discussion of the personage Satan). It is enough to add here that the conjunction of Jesus with the Temple (more exactly with the top of the Temple) is in the text a metonymic figure which will become especially meaningful at the end of the gospels: what happens to Jesus prefigures what will happen to the Temple (cf. the eschatological discourses). Furthermore, the disjunction of Jesus from the Temple in Matt 24:1 which announces the death of the one and the ruin of the other anticipates the exit from the earthly plan and the return in glory of the Son of Man. This simply suggests that the place occupied by Jesus is pertinent for the meaning of the narrative. It can be expressed in the following categories: "localized vs. non-localized," "conjointed with the Temple vs. disjointed from the Temple," "here vs. there," "up vs. down." The relation of Jesus to the location is therefore something to take into account here as well as in the whole Gospel, and we shall see how it is combined with other semantic features of the personage.

Set on the top of the Temple, Jesus is in an ambiguous situation, and thus an unstable situation. As other texts will emphasize (cf. Matt 21:42; Matt 23:37-39 for the relation of Jesus-Jerusalem), Jesus is at the place where he belongs and which guarantees the completion and stability of the Jewish institution. When this position will be recognized and guaranteed as his, the work of God will reach its end — "It was the stone rejected by the builders that became the keystone. This was the Lord's doing and it is wonderful to see" (Matt 21:42 quoting Ps 118:22-23). Jerusalem is consecrated and, metaphorically, it is the Temple which Satan has just completed by setting the keystone at its place, the top of the edifice.

From a different perspective, the metonymic and in part

metaphoric relation (a "metaphoro-metonymic relation," as Louis Marin says; cf. *Sémiotique de la Passion*, pp. 51-52) which assigns a meaning to the conjunction Jesus-Temple affects also the complementary relations with contiguous elements, Temple-Holy City and Jerusalem-Jewish community. Jesus, the "keystone" must also be set at the head of the community: he is its "head." It is precisely this which Satan proposes. The movement in space is nothing other than a figure of his accession to the messianic throne. The quotation of Psalm 91 suggests this, even though the text is not directly and exclusively messianic. Thus, a decisive step must still be taken so that Jesus might reach his true place — the "throne of David his father." Any metaphor and any metonomy would be abolished by perfect coincidence of the project with its realization. It is not a fall which is proposed to Jesus, but an ascension; not a jump in space but the last step of history. The process of history would be transformed into its completed state. It would be the end, in the sense of the Greek word, *telos*.

It is understandable that this borderline situation might be especially revelatory of the values of signification hidden by the name of Jesus. The temporal categories parallel to the spatial categories are themselves pertinent: "time in process vs. beyond time," "immediate end vs. continuation of the unfolding of time." These categories are further combined with the ethnic categories, "Jewishness vs. universality." For, indeed, Satan's proposition presupposes a fulfillment of God's work in the framework of Judaism. The return to Jerusalem from the wilderness emphasizes this point, as does the contrast with the third temptation "on a very high mountain." At this prominent place which Scripture itself recognizes as Jesus' place, is raised the question which was already at the center of the first temptation: should what is possible be appropriated here and now? Should a need for acknowledgment be satisfied here and now even though it might extinguish a wider desire? Or, on the contrary, should Jesus go "elsewhere" and wait until "later" for a universal acknowledgment? Where is the high place which is prepared for the true manifestation of the Son of God? Before which crowd gathered in front of which Temple?

When he refuses the proposition of the tempter, Jesus reorganizes these semantic values into classes. Once more it is clear that the manifestation of the textual content takes place at the level of these "suprasegment" units; they are the actual building-blocks of meaning. It is on these units that are performed the various operations on the surface by the movements and the actions of the actors and not on the coded signified of each lexeme.

Jesus did not refuse the movement which brings him to the Holy City and to the Temple. During his life he will not refuse it, either. At times, he will even emphasize the priority given to Israel in the history of salvation (cf. Matt 15:21-28, the healing of the daughter of a Canaanite woman). His response to Satan distinguishes his presence in Jerusalem and at the Temple from his immediate accession to the Davidic throne. From the top of the Temple to the head of the community of Israel, there is one step which Jesus refuses to take. "As for seats at my right hand and my left, these are not mine to grant . . . " (Matt 21-23). From one signifier to another, if meaning must indeed follow this metonymic path, the movement must not be hurried. Timing is important, and the delays fixed by the Father are also part of the human condition. The relationship between Jesus and the Temple must be established by a patient courtship without constraint, without proud elevation of the mind and of the heart. The encounter will take place (and has already taken place according to the customs of his people, the Law of Moses in Luke 2:22) according to the circumstances, the possibilities, and the necessities of life. Thus, at one level Jesus' relation to Jerusalem is similar to that of any other Israelite. Of course, on other grounds everything is different for Jesus who comes here to his Father's home, yet even this difference will be apprehended only spiritually and without constraint. Between Jesus and the Temple, the relation is one of reciprocal "service." The Temple must be given back to the Father, i.e., returned to its spiritual function. "According to

Scripture," he said, "my house will be called a house of prayer" (Matt 21:13). It is not the footstool of the messianic throne. It is in it and not above it that Jesus has his place. It is the echo of his word in the Temple which must manifest his identity: "He had gone into the Temple and was teaching . . . " (Matt 21:23).

What will come out of this relationship? What the Father wants, and also what men want . . . Jesus knows that the Temple is his place, his domain. He knows that in it he is truly himself and that he will be recognized only when he will be in the shadow of the Temple or in its light. He needs the Temple in order to fulfill his mission. But will he overtake it, assault it, close his hands on these stones so that the Temple might become the price of his triumph? Once more, this would be confusing the satisfied need with the desire. It would be denying the unsuspected potentialities of this relation to the Temple. It would be refusing to let himself be slowly molded so as to welcome the true Temple which this one, below him, represents but also hides and distorts. It is a matter of his relationship to the Father and to mankind, and therefore it concerns his manifestation as Son.

First, his relationship to the Father is at stake. From the Father, he must receive the Temple as part of himself, as domain, as heritage. In terms of the Temple of stones, this means that Jesus must receive it exactly as the sons of the people of Israel do. If, one day, for his Son, God wants to build another Temple which would be truly his own and be the seat of his royal power, it will be only as a response to the loyal acceptance of "the Law of the Temple of stones," i.e., because Jesus thrown down from the top of the Temple will have agreed to be broken on the ground, stone among the stones of a ruin, on account of men's fault. Then his filial identity will be manifested in that he will not have tempted the Lord; he will not have asked that the laws of nature and of history work in his favor.

It can be noted that the sonship is again reflected in the quotation from Deuteronomy, "You must not put the Lord your God to the test." The twofold use of the second person as linguistic manifestation of the interlocutor is a mark of the enunciation.

Somebody speaks to somebody else; the knowledge of this situation of enunciation is necessary in order to determine the value of the "you." Let us leave aside the question of knowing how in the Jewish reading of Deuteronomy the relationship between the enunciator (Moses?) and the receiver (the people) was understood. When Jesus repeats the traditional interdiction and addresses it to Satan, the universal value of the "you" does not disappear. To any man and, therefore, to Jesus who wants to be totally a man, it is said, "you must not put the Lord to the test." But a new value is superimposed upon it: "You, Satan, you must not put the Lord to the test." It could not be better said without falling into the diabolic trap, that the refusal to demonstrate here and now the divine sonship was the only possible way to secure the true manifestation. Once more, Jesus prefers the truth to the apparent exactitude.

In this temptation, Jesus' relation to men is also at stake. The freedom that Jesus keeps vis-à-vis this Temple by sacrificing its privileges is also distance vis-à-vis the Jewish institution and the national messianism. Because he is Son of God, Jesus is not tied down to this Temple of stones, to this holy city, to this sacred center of the universe. What would be valuable, satisfying, exact in this acclamation of the Messiah by the Jewish people, would be radically distorted by the hopeless ignorance in which the rest of the world would be maintained. Jesus has chosen between particularism and universalism, and already this place appears as too narrow, too confined. As the Gospel according to John expresses it, " . . . the hour will come — in fact it is here already — when true worshippers will worship the Father in spirit and truth . . . You will worship the Father neither on this mountain nor in Jerusalem . . . " (John 4:21-23). As John explains it, what Jesus says about the Temple refers to his own body (John 2:21).

Here we reach the second signifier which represents Jesus' identity. What the Word was in the first temptation, the *body* is in the second. The term, "body," is not used, but the semantic content is present. This is easily verified by noting the metonymies of the body in Satan's discourse, " . . . throw *yourself* down . . . they support *you* on their hands in case you hurt your *foot* against a stone." The relation Temple-body is therefore on the horizon of the text and the metaphor, Temple-body, is substituted for the metonymy, "Temple-Jesus as keystone." Everything which is said about the Temple of stones is also said more truthfully about the body. It is here, in this human, fleshly condition of Jesus, that the word of Scripture takes all its value: "You shall not put to the test the Lord your God" or "You think that I cannot appeal to my Father who would promptly send more than twelve legions of angels?" Jesus will say to Peter in Matt 26:53.

In concluding this analysis of the second temptation, it is useful to review the semantic categories used in it. The personage of Jesus is essentially composed of the following elements: "time, delay, accepted lateness, " "common condition," "universality, free relation to the 'place' (privileged corporeal signifier)," "accepted separation from the Temple so as to enter another place," "divine sonship suggested but not demonstrated, expected in the suppression of the corporeal signifier" . . . "I tell you solemnly, not a single stone here will be left on another: everything will be destroyed . . . The coming of the Son of Man will be like lightning striking in the east and flashing far into the west . . . " (Matt 24:2 and 24:27).

Power and Force

As we have already suggested, the third temptation operates in relation to another more global object. The gap which separates this object from the messianic acknowledgment in Israel reproduces somehow the semantic difference, "Judaism vs. universality," but in caricature. This caricature is sufficient confirmation of the presence of these categories in the semantic field.

The mountain upon which Satan transports Jesus is determined and defined only by its function as observatory. The Temple and the mountain are related to each other in terms of status, "cultural and built, a signifier in a national and religious system (inclusion of the Temple in Jerusalem)" vs. "natural and outside any human activities." On the religious axis, the Temple is "marked" and the mountain "non-marked." From this observation we can derive the features "Judaism" for the Temple vs. "undifferentiated world" for the mountain. After the wilderness, the location of the separation from the differentiations provoked by man's presence and after the Temple, the heart of the Jewish city, the mountain represents a position related to universality in its earthly and political manifestation above the national distinction, i.e., a position of domination by sight.

What can be the relation of Jesus to this place? From there he can see, as Satan shows them to him, all of the kingdoms of the earth with their splendor. It is in terms of what he sees down there that he must decide. The elevation on the mountain is therefore purely utilitarian and is immediately cancelled by the downward direction of the sight, and by the downward movement which would be necessary in order to take possession of the kingdoms. The "fall at Satan's feet" reproduces on another stage the same movement. Thus, we should not view the mountain as a metaphor of actual elevation. Just as there is reflection of a landscape in water, so also the mountain as inverse elevation represents the complete immersion in the earthly and human realm. Jesus is confronted here with human ways and realizations. As a man among men, he will not ignore any of this. From Palestine which he will never leave, he will have knowledge of the other nations, of the kingdoms and empires. His universalist aim will demand that he recognize, define, and manifest himself in relation with the human condition in its wider generality. The mountain is the mountain of knowledge, the mountain of the universal message (Matt 5:1) and of the new Law, the mountain of the manifestation of the filial identity (Matt 17:1-8, the transfiguration), the mountain of the universal mission: "All authority . . . has been given me . . . Go, therefore, make disciples of all the nations . . ." (Matt 28:16-20). From one mountain to the other is affirmed the same breaking out of Judaism and the same reaching out toward men of all nations and conditions.

But, like the Temple, the mountain is an ambiguous place: Jesus must manifest what are the true values crystallized around it. "From knowledge to possesion (or from seeing to possessing)" — such could be the title of this passage. Seeing the reality opens the space of hunger. On the axis of domination and political power, for the one who has refused the throne of David, the universal kingship might be "pleasing to the eye" (Genesis 3:6) and seem "good to take." It might even seem useful for the fulfillment of the salvific mission. For, indeed, it is not in order to *see* the reality that Jesus has come but in order to transform it, not in order to contemplate from the top of the mountain the human drama, but in order to play a decisive role in it. Yet, it is still a matter of taking the step which separates the preparation from the performance, the "marche d'approche" from the victorious struggle. This step is possible here and now.

But how? Who would this universal king be who would suddenly enter the world with all the emblems of the supreme power? Who would be designated as sovereign before signifying himself as such? The Son of God? Of course not! It is not from the Father that he would receive his power, since he would be separated forever from God because of his worshiping Satan. And, as soon as he would have become king by falling at the feet of the invisible *anti-sender*, his program would have nothing to do with freedom and truth. Once more, the haste for reaching the proposed object would lead to the negation of the deep aspiration, to the suppression of the other possibilities opened by the situation, to the fatal emptying of the program in which Jesus is involved. There are better ways to be among men after climbing down from the observatory-mountain. "After he had come down from the mountain large crowds followed him. A leper now came up . . ." (Matt 8:1-2). "As they came down from the mountain Jesus gave them this order, 'Tell no one about the vision until the Son of Man has risen from the dead'" (Matt 17:9).

In fact, Jesus' response in our text suggests only indirectly that Jesus will be among men. The response has two parts — the injunction to Satan, "Be off . . . " and the quotation of Deut 6:13. For the first time, the enunciation is marked without ambiguity outside of the quotation (the situation is different in Luke's text) by the second person. It is an order. He to whom this order is addressed is in a subordinated position. He who gives this order, although he is not formally manifested in the text, designates himself in position of domination. This is the inversion of "If you fall at my feet," and thus the implicit affirmation that he who refuses earthly power is indeed the actual universal sovereign. This is further emphasized by the fact that Jesus becomes the *sender*, who assigns roles including Satan's role. The equality with God and the divine sonship are thus manifested as the implicit signified of this brief discourse.

Regarding the question of enunciation, the quotation is to be analyzed just as the quotation of Deut 6:16 in Matt 4:7 has been. Jesus sets himself among those who receive this normative word. At the same time Jesus suggests that when men (and perhaps even Satan himself as a rebellious participant) read this text, they should define Jesus exclusively in terms of his relation to "the Lord your God." Apparently this response refutes only the clause, ". . . if you fall at my feet and worship me." The acquisition of the universal kingship seems to remain undetermined. Jesus would define himself exclusively in terms of the "rights of God." He is the champion of God's rights. What about *power*?

It is noteworthy that Jesus first manifests his power by immediately sending Satan away. For this he does not need to climb down from the mountain! The refusal of political domination is accompanied by a power over Satan. The orientation of the power is pertinent — "over men vs. over Satan (and the various forms of evil)," "dominating power vs. healing power." The casting out of demons manifests the pertinence of these oppositions. This orientation of the power is also another figure of worship of God; it is conditioned by the acceptance of the end without appropriating it for oneself. Each of these manifestations will reveal the filial identity that Jesus acknowledges and assumes. Thus, Jesus does not refuse *power*. With *Word*, and *body*, the power is the third signifier which manifests Jesus' relation to the Father. Just as Word and body are not signifieds in and of themselves, so also with power. The power simultaneously reveals the signified and hides it. The power is not absolute and final. The day will come when the series of three signifiers will have to be cancelled, suspended, so that the filial signified might be manifested in its purity. For, indeed, the signifiers must submit to the interference of events which transforms them. The Father and men will dispose of these signifiers. Men will suspend them, believing in so doing they can suppress the revelation of the Son and avoid the risk it involves. The Father will substitute for these signifiers the complete and final object which is designated by these figures and which Jesus expects. Then the Word will have become bread, the body a spiritual Temple, and the healing power, a power of resurrection and of universal renewal. Then men will know that in Jesus God is present.

D. CONCLUSION

Not everything has been said about the semiotic function of this text and even less has been said about its semantic content. Nevertheless, the preceding analysis permits an evaluation of the method we have used. This was our goal. We especially need to verify the coherence of the two approaches and the operational character of the semantic analysis. This second part has been longer and more detailed in order to compensate for the brevity of our theoretical presentation on the semantic analysis. Three remarks are appropriate:

1. The presentation of the semantic contents which has been purposefully organized around the two main actors might have seemed, at times, a return to the psychological perspective which we had excluded at the outset. Some of our formulations might have suggested that we were concerned to present the interplay of feelings, reflections, hesitations, decisions generated within Jesus by Satan's propositions. In fact, we were dealing with something quite different. We were concerned with grasping through the narrative network the semantic values of the forms of non-lexematic units — pre- or meta-lexematic units. We attempted to show how these semantic units function on the basis of the system we had found in the text in our analysis of the narrative structure. Yet, in order to facilitate the presentation of this semantic analysis, we had to use synthetic and descriptive figurations and

formulations even though they seemed to refer to psychological features. These formulations, which might seem to refer to intellectual and psychological operations of Jesus (and also, at times, of Satan), represent in fact the interplay of semantic features in the *reader's* or analyst's mind. They are never an attempt to represent what Jesus could think. It is to help understand how the *text* functions that our comments have been written — not to facilitate access to that to which the text refers.

2. The main purpose of this second part of our analysis was to determine the level of the signified at which the semantic analysis must be carried out in order to take advantage of the results of the narrative (or syntactic) analysis. Here is the value and the weakness of this work. We have systematically excluded the lexematic level; the analysis of the words in themselves has no place in the preceding comments. It is above the "code" of the language (*langue*) that we can hope to find the main values of the content which are at work in the discourse. We must renounce the simple use of the dictionary and must define another level of semantic investigation. Thus, we understand our attempt to reconstruct the content of the personages on the basis of values which are not manifested but are, nevertheless, suggested by the general dynamics of the text and confirmed by broad correlations with elements of the complete Gospel corpus. The criterion of pertinence that we used was not so much the presence of these categories in the various lexemes of the text but, rather, their compatibility with the emerging meaning of features recorded in the dictionary *and* the narrative models. We have taken the risk of performing our analysis at a level of generalization too far above the text in order to make clear the difference between this semantic analysis and the traditional semic analysis which is so close to the surface of the text that it deals with isolated elements of the text. Our analysis might have gone too far in this generalization, yet it has to be understood as a project which attempts to establish the semantic analysis of text at a level in which it can become operational.

3. We have not formalized the results of our analysis in order to

make it clear that the formalization of the results has to wait for further verifications of the pertinence of the categories we have used. The verification would demand the construction of various models and especially the logical model (logical "square" or "hexagon") which would explicitly show what are the possible combinations on the basis of the oppositions. This necessary additional step of the analysis would then permit a more precise identification of the configurations of the text.

This verification would entail a detailed analysis of the whole Gospel corpus. It is the comparison of the models found in various parts of the text and the formulation of the transformations of these models which would lead us to the *structure*. For this purpose we need to carry out more partial analyses. Louis Marin's work already provides precious elements and the general framework for such a task.